T0040190

Best
Practices
for
Elementary
Classrooms

More Books by Randi Stone

Best Practices for Teaching Reading: What Award-Winning Classroom Teachers Do, 2008

Best Practices for Teaching Social Studies: What Award-Winning Classroom Teachers Do, 2008

Best Practices for Teaching Writing: What Award-Winning Classroom Teachers Do, 2007

Best Practices for Teaching Mathematics: What Award-Winning Classroom Teachers Do, 2007

Best Practices for Teaching Science: What Award-Winning Classroom Teachers Do, 2007

Best Classroom Management Practices for Reaching All Learners: What Award-Winning Classroom Teachers Do, 2005

Best Teaching Practices for Reaching All Learners: What Award-Winning Classroom Teachers Do, 2004

What?! Another New Mandate? What Award-Winning Teachers Do When School Rules Change, 2002

Best Practices for High School Classrooms: What Award-Winning Secondary Teachers Do, 2001

Best Classroom Practices: What Award-Winning Elementary Teachers Do, 1999

New Ways to Teach Using Cable Television: A Step-by-Step Guide, 1997

Best Practices for Elementary Classrooms

What Award-Winning Teachers Do

RANDI STONE

Skyhorse Publishing

Copyright © 2009 by Randi Stone

First Skyhorse Publishing edition 2015.

All rights reserved. No part of this book may be reproduced in any manner without the express written consent of the publisher, except in the case of brief excerpts in critical reviews or articles. All inquiries should be addressed to Skyhorse Publishing, 307 West 36th Street, 11th Floor, New York, NY 10018.

Skyhorse Publishing books may be purchased in bulk at special discounts for sales promotion, corporate gifts, fund-raising, or educational purposes. Special editions can also be created to specifications. For details, contact the Special Sales Department, Skyhorse Publishing, 307 West 36th Street, 11th Floor, New York, NY 10018 or info@skyhorsepublishing.com.

Skyhorse® and Skyhorse Publishing® are registered trademarks of Skyhorse Publishing, Inc.®, a Delaware corporation.

Visit our website at www.skyhorsepublishing.com.

10 9 8 7 6 5 4 3 2 1

Library of Congress Cataloging-in-Publication Data is available on file.

Cover design by Michael Dubowe

Print ISBN: 978-1-63220-542-1
Ebook ISBN: 978-1-63220-959-7

Printed in the United States of America

Contents

Preface

My goal of helping teachers has remained the same for over a decade. I have introduced teachers from across the United States to the best practices in elementary schools. The success of *Best Classroom Practices: What Award-Winning Elementary Teachers Do* has led to *MORE Best Practices for Elementary Teachers: What Award-Winning Teachers Do.* This book provides teachers with a new smorgasbord of information.

There is endless information out there and it can take hours to find just what you are looking for. This book makes it easy. It is full of valuable lessons from outstanding teachers. These teachers are the ones highlighted in journals and magazines and the ones who win grants, fellowships, and contests. These are the Teachers of the Year, National Educator Award winners, recipients of the Milken Family Foundation award, and ING Unsung Heroes—and the list continues. I wanted to talk to them and hear about what they are doing. I wanted to know what makes them outstanding and what they are doing in their classrooms.

This book is the product of sharing at its best and is organized in four parts. Part I highlights classroom practices across the curriculum. Topics include classroom management, creative scheduling, community involvement, differentiating instruction, and using technology in classrooms. A sample of the lessons in Part I are *Building the Atmosphere, Differentiation Using Story Cubes,* and *Technology for a Varied and More Interesting Classroom.* Part II focuses on science and math. Lessons include *Using Mysteries to Teach Science Inquiry* and *Math-A-Thon.* Part III addresses teaching reading and writing. *Nonfiction Guided Reading Lesson* and *Multigenre Writing* are just a few of the practices addressed. Finally, Part IV has a variety of lessons on social studies, music, art, and physical education, spanning topics like *Cultural Diversity in Our Community: Past and Present, Inaugural Poetry Through Elementary School Publications,* and *Celebrating Music.*

I hope you enjoy each submission with the same enthusiasm and excitement that I did. Thanks to the tremendously giving educators across the United States, *Best Practices for Elementary Classrooms: What Award-Winning Teachers Do* will give you an inside view of education practices and exemplary lesson plans.

About the Author

 **Randi Stone** is a graduate of Clark University, Boston University, and Salem State College. She completed her doctorate in education at the University of Massachusetts, Lowell. She is the author of 15 books, including her series *Best Practices for Teaching Reading: What Award-Winning Teachers Do; Best Practices for Teaching Social Studies: What Award-Winning Teachers Do; Best Practices for Teaching Writing: What Award-Winning Teachers Do; Best Practices for Teaching Mathematics: What Award-Winning Teachers Do;* and *Best Practices for Teaching Science: What Award-Winning Teachers Do.* She lives with her teenage daughter, Blair, in Keene, New Hampshire.

About the Contributors

Frieda Taylor Aiken, Gifted Teacher, Jackson Elementary School
E-mail: friedaa@bellsouth.net

Number of years teaching: 20
Awards: Toyota Tapestry Mini Grant, Environmental Science Education,
"Ecology in a Box," 2005; Teacher of the Year, Jackson
Elementary School, 2000–2001; District V Georgia Science
Teacher of the Year, 2000–2001

Maranda Alcalá, English Language Development Specialist, Salish
Ponds Elementary School
E-mail: marandaalcala@msn.com

Number of years teaching: 9
Award: American Star of Teaching Award, Department of
Education, 2006

Luella L. Atkins, Reading Specialist/Reading First Program Literacy
Coach, Airport Elementary School
E-mail: latkins@fergflor.k12.mo.us or luellaatkins@aol.com

Number of years teaching: 11
Awards: Excellence in Education, St. Louis American Foundation,
2007; Milken Family Foundation National Educator Award,
2006; Apple for the Teacher, Iota Phi Lambda Sorority,
Inc., 2005

Brandy Bailey, Fourth-Grade Language Arts, Oak Grove Central
Elementary
E-mail: brandy.bailey@desotocountyschools.org

xiv BEST PRACTICES FOR ELEMENTARY CLASSROOMS

Number of years teaching: 12
Award: No Child Left Behind American Star Teaching Award, 2006

KJ Bailey, Second-Grade Teacher, Sallie Jones Elementary School
E-mail: girlwonder713@gmail.com

Number of years teaching: 5
Awards: Veterans of Foreign Wars National Citizenship Educational
Teacher of the Year for the State of Florida, 2008; Veterans
of Foreign Wars National Citizenship Educational Teacher
of the Year for the District of Charlotte County, 2007;
Veterans of Foreign Wars National Citizenship Educational
Teacher of the Year for the Post, 2007

Eileen Biegel, Fifth-Grade Team Leader/Teacher, R. M. Paterson
E-mail: ecbiegel@mail.clay.k12.fl.us or biegelfamily89@yahoo.com

Years of teaching: 9
Awards: National Board Certified Teacher (Middle Childhood
Generalist), 2007; ING Unsung Heroes Award, 2007

Peggy J. Billiard, Elementary Teacher-Librarian, Columbia Elementary
School
E-mail: billiardp@lcsc.k12.in.us or peggybilliard@aol.com

Number of years teaching: 35
Awards: Veterans of Foreign Wars National Citizenship Education
Teacher Award, Indiana, 2008; National Education Asso-
ciation Foundation Award for Teaching Excellence, National
Selection Panel Final Ten Awardee, 2007–2008; Horace
Mann/Indiana State Teachers' Association, Hoosier Educator
Teacher Award, Indiana, 2007; Applebee's All-American
Award for Teachers, 2007

Renee Borden, Kindergarten Teacher, A.B. Hill Elementary
E-mail: krkb02@yahoo.com

Number of years teaching: 20
Awards: Milken Family Foundation National Educator Award, 2006;
Outstanding Literacy Development Award for Memphis
City Schools, 2005; National Board Certification, 2004

Karen Ann Brown, Instructional Coach, Shelton Elementary School
>   E-mail: karbrown@jeffco.k12.co.us
>
>   *Number of years teaching:* 15
>   *Award:* Milken Family Foundation National Educator Award, 2006

Carol Brueggeman, Science/Math Resource Teacher, Mark Twain Elementary
>   E-mail: bruegc@d11.org
>
>   *Number of years teaching:* 29
>   *Awards:* The Presidential Award for Excellence in Math and Science Teaching, 2006; Colorado Association of Science Teachers, President, 2005–2008; NSF–STEP-UP Science Resource Teacher, 2000–2006

Nancy Bryant, Therapeutic BED Teacher, Supply Elementary
>   E-mail: nbryant@bcswan.net
>
>   *Number of years teaching:* 11
>   *Award:* ATMC Smart Connections Grant, 2007; Star News Future Corps Award, 2007; Toshiba American Foundation, 2006; Best Buy Teach Award, 2006

Pam Cyr, Fifth-Grade Teacher, Shelburne Community School
>   E-mail: pcyr@cssu.org
>
>   *Number of years teaching:* 15
>   *Award:* Milken Family Foundation National Educator Award, 2006

Stacy Gardner Dibble, Fifth-Grade Teacher, Prairie Elementary
>   E-mail: Stacy.Dibble@ISD518.net
>
>   *Number of years teaching:* 18
>   *Award:* ING Unsung Heroes Award, 2005

Debbie Easley, Fifth-Grade Teacher, Priceville Elementary School
>   E-mail: debeasley@aol.com or dceasley@morgank12.org
>
>   *Number of years teaching:* 21

Awards: NSTA Distinguished Elementary Teacher Award, 2007; NSTA Delta Excellence in Teaching Elementary Inquiry-Based Science Education Award, 2006; Alabama Science Teacher's Association—Outstanding Elementary Science Teacher of the Year, 2005–2006

Barb A. Egbert, Kindergarten Teacher, Franklin Elementary
E-mail: egbertb@cape.k12.mo.us

Number of years teaching: 26
Awards: Presidential Award for Excellence in Mathematics Teaching, 2006; Cape Girardeau Chamber of Commerce Teacher of the Year, 2000

Michael Flynn, Second-Grade Teacher, William E. Norris Elementary School
E-mail: mflynn.ward7@gmail.com

Number of years teaching: 10
Awards: Massachusetts Teacher of the Year, 2008; Local Heroes Award from the Ronald McDonald House Charities, 2008; Teacher Excellence Award from Smart Technologies, 2008

Debbie Gordon, Third-Grade Teacher, Madison Simis
E-mail: dgordon@msd38.org

Number of years teaching: 23
Awards: Presidential Award for Excellence in Teaching Mathematics and Science, 2002; Madison District You Make a Difference Award, 1998; Madison School District Teacher of the Year, 1996

Deb Guthrie, Second-Grade Teacher, Valentine Hills School
E-mail: dguthrie@ties2.net

Number of years teaching: 23
Awards: Presidential Award for Excellence in Mathematics and Science Teaching, 2006; Christa McAuliffe Fellowship, 2001–2002; National Board Certified Teacher, 1999

Lisa M. Hall, Title I Mathematics Specialist, Jacob L. Adams Elementary School

E-mail: Lmhall@henrico.k12.va.us

Number of years teaching: 22

Awards: Presidential Award for Excellence in Mathematics and Science Teaching, 2006; National Board Certification, Early Adolescence/Mathematics, 2006; Michael Jordan Fundamentals Grant, 2005

Kim Heckart, Third-Grade Teacher, Prairie Ridge Elementary

E-mail: kheckart@prairiepride.org

Number of years teaching: 18

Awards: National Outstanding Social Studies Teacher of the Year, 2007; Iowa Social Studies Teacher of the Year, 2007; Gilder Lehrman Iowa History Teacher of the Year, 2007

Kelli Higgins, Third-Grade Teacher, Bolin Elementary School

E-mail: higginsk@epd86.org

Number of years teaching: 12

Awards: Toshiba American Foundation, 2007; STEM—Science Technology Engineering and Mathematics Grant (Bradley University), 2006; East Peioria Education Foundation, 2006

Cindy L. Hodgeson, Adaptive Physical Education Specialist, Agua Calient Elementary and Tanque Verde Elementary

Number of years teaching: 27

Awards: ING Unsung Heroes Award, 2007; Arizona State Board of Education: Golden Bell Award, 1997

Karin Huttsell, First-Grade Teacher, Hickory Center Elementary

E-mail: karin.huttsell@nacs.k12.in.us

Number of years teaching: 31

Awards: ING Unsung Heroes Award, 2007; ITT Excellence in Education Grant, 2006; Earthwatch Fellowship, 2006

Jodi Jari, ESL Teacher, Merrill Elementary School
E-mail: jodjar@oshkosh.k12.wi.us

Number of years teaching: 18
Awards: Who's Who Among America's Teachers, 2006; American Star of Teaching—National Award, 2005

Dr. Kendra Jiles, Generic Self-Contained Teacher (Kindergarten–Fifth-Grade), Maryville Elementary School
E-mail: kendrajiles@aol.com

Number of years teaching: 12
Awards: Teacher of the Month, 2006; National Board Certified Teacher, Exceptional Needs Specialist, 2004; Maryville Elementary School Teacher of the Year, 2004

Tammy Haggerty Jones, Third-Grade Teacher, Strassburg School
E-mail: upontheroof24@comcast.net

Number of years teaching: 6
Awards: National-Louis University R.E.A.C.H. Career Achievement Award, 2006; Japan Fulbright Memorial Fund, 2005; DisneyHand Teacher Award, 2004

Shari Kaneshiro, Fifth-Grade Teacher, Hokulani Elementary School
E-mail: sharikaneshiro@gmail.com

Number of years teaching: 14
Awards: Presidential Award for Excellence in Mathematics and Science Teaching Awardee, 2006; Honolulu District Teacher of the Year, 2004; Presidential Award for Excellence in Mathematics and Science Teaching Science Finalist, 2002

Elizabeth Grelle Kruse, Kindergarten Teacher, Frances Xavier Warde School
E-mail: grellee@fxw.org

Number of years teaching: 13
Award: Kohl McCormick Early Childhood Teaching Award, 2007

Ganna Maymind, First-Grade Teacher, Asher Holmes Elementary School
E-mail: ganna15@hotmail.com

Number of years teaching: 7
Awards: New Jersey Governor's Teacher Recognition Program Honoree, 2008; Donald Graves Award for Excellence in the Teaching of Writing, National Council of Teachers of English, 2005

Helen Melvin, Retired Second-Grade Teacher (June 2007); Adjunct Professor, Dr. Levesque School; University of Maine at Fort Kent
E-mail: h_melvin@hotmail.com or Helen.Melvin@maine.edu

Number of years teaching: 37
Awards: Who's Who Among American Teachers and Educators, 2005–2007; Who's Who in America, 2004–2005; National SemiConductor Internet Innovator Award, 2002

Ginger Mendenhall, Instructional Facilitator, Tulsa Public Schools
E-mail: mendegi@tulsaschools.org

Number of years teaching: 16
Awards: National Education Association Excellence in Teaching, 2006–2007; David Boren Medal of Excellence in Teaching, 2003–2004; Milken Family Foundation National Educator Award, 2000–2001

Susan Menkes, Art Teacher (Kindergarten–Fifth Grade), Cantiague Elementary School
E-mail: artnsoul12@aol.com

Number of years of teaching: 17
Award: All-USA Teacher Team, 2006

Diana A. Minor, Special Services Teacher, Eugene Field Elementary
E-mail: dminor@hannibal.k12.mo.us

Number of years teaching: 25
Award: Mark Twain Creative Teaching Award, 2007; ING Unsung Heroes Award, 2007; District Teacher of the Year, 2001

Marianne Morin, AIS Reading and Math Teacher, Watkins Glen Elementary School
> E-mail: morinmom@yahoo.com

> *Number of years teaching:* 29
> *Awards:* Time Warner National Teachers Award, 2006; Parent Teachers Association Educator of the Year, 2004–2005

LeAnn Morris, MEd, Technology Teacher, Empire Elementary
> E-mail: lmorris@carson.k12.nv.us

> *Number of years teaching:* 18
> *Awards:* National Education Association I CAN Learn Award for Teaching Excellence, 2008; Three-Year Appointment from the Governor of Nevada to serve as a member on the Commission on Educational Excellence for the state of Nevada, 2008; Nevada Teacher of the Year, 2008

Amy Nicholl, Fifth-Grade Teacher, Skyview Elementary
> E-mail: anicholl@windsor.k12.co.us

> *Number of years teaching:* 29
> *Awards:* Delta Education/Frey-Neo/CPO Science Education Awards for Excellence in Inquiry-based Science Teaching, 2007; Shell Outstanding Science Educator, Semi-Finalist, 2007; Presidential Award for Excellence in Mathematics and Science Teaching, 2000

Tony Nichols, Kindergarten Teacher, Cherry River Elementary
> E-mail: tonytown@verizon.net

> *Number of years teaching:* 23
> *Awards:* USA Today Teacher Team, 2008; West Virginia Teacher of the Year Finalist, 2004 and 2007; National Board Certified Teacher, 2005

Reid Nunn, Fourth-Grade and Fifth-Grade Multiage, McCollum
> E-mail: nunn_r@aps.edu

Number of years teaching: 12

Award: Milken Family Foundation National Educator Award, 2006

Denese Odegaard, String Specialist
E-mail: denese@cableone.net

Number of years teaching: 25

Awards: ASTA Citation for Leadership and Merit, 2006 and 2008; Lois Bailey Glenn Award for Teaching Excellence from the National Music Foundation, 2006; North Dakota String Teacher of the Year, 2005

Andrea Payan, Teacher, Morgandale School
E-mail: payanar@milwaukee.k12.wi.us

Number of years teaching: 8

Award: Milken Family Foundation National Educator Award, 2006

Sue Davis Pope, Fifth- and Sixth-Grade Teacher and Math Coordinator, Westridge Elementary
E-mail: suep@provo.edu

Number of years teaching: 13

Awards: Milken Family Foundation National Educator Award, 2006; Building on Excellence Award, Provo School District Foundation, 2006; Pride of Westridge, Teacher of the Year, 1999, 2002, 2006

Heather E. Robinson, Fifth-Grade Teacher, Desert Canyon Elementary School
E-mail: hrobinson@susd.org

Number of years teaching: 15

Awards: Arizona History Teacher of the Year, Gilder Lehrman Institute of American History, 2006; Distinguished Teaching Achievement Award, National Council for Geographic Education, 2002; Excellence in Education and Technology Award, Cox Communications, 1997

Nikki Salvatico, First-Grade Teacher, General Wayne Elementary School

> *Number of years teaching:* 12
> *Awards:* Pennsylvania Teacher of the Year, 2005; USA Today Teacher Team Award, 2005

Christopher R. Shadle, Third-Grade Teacher, Self-Contained, L. J. Smith Elementary School
E-mail: cshadle@massillon.sparcc.org

> *Number of years teaching:* 27
> *Awards:* National Geographic Society Education Foundation Grant, 2005; NEA Innovation Grant, 2004; Ohio Arts Council Integration Project, 2003, 2004

Marianne Sipe, Second-Grade Teacher, Old Center Elementary
E-mail: amsipe1@yahoo.com

> *Number of years teaching:* 16
> *Awards:* Toshiba America Foundation, 2006; Nashville Metropolitan Schools Mini-Grant, 2002; Tennessee Space Week, "Space Readers," 2001

Wendy Smith, Kindergarten–Fifth-Grade Math, Science, Technology Specialist, Klem Road South Elementary School
E-mail: wendy_smith@websterschools.org

> *Number of years teaching:* 15
> *Awards:* HP Technology for Teaching Grant 2007–2008; Best Buy Regional Teach Grant Award for Technology Inspired Teaching, 2007; National Science Teachers Association/Vernier Technology Award, 2007

Tammy Spratt, Fifth-Grade Teacher, Carson Elementary
E-mail: tjspratt@laca.org

> *Number of years teaching:* 18
> *Awards:* Kentucky Elementary Teacher of the Year, 2008; Kentucky's Preserve American History Teacher of the

Year, 2007; Kentucky Council for the Social Studies Outstanding Teacher of the Year, 2007

Sharla Steever, Third-Grade Teacher, Hill City Elementary
E-mail: ssteever@hillcity.k12.sd.us

Number of years teaching: 8
Awards: Japan Fulbright Memorial Fellowship, SD Alternate, 2008; Presidential Award for Excellence in Math and Science Teaching, 2007; Hill City Teacher of the Year, 2006

Kim Tredick, Fifth-Grade Teacher, Sulphur Springs Community School
E-mail: kimmy-jo@sbcglobal.net

Number of years teaching: 20
Awards: Milken Family Foundation National Educator Award, 2007; Sulphur Springs School Teacher of the year, 2006; Sulphur Springs School District Teachers' Association Teacher of the Year, 2006

PART I

Classroom Practices Across the Curriculum

Classroom Management, Scheduling, and Community Involvement

Overview, Chapters 1–4

1. **Elizabeth Grelle Kruse,** a kindergarten teacher in Chicago, shows us how she builds a productive learning environment in her kindergarten classroom. Elizabeth's invaluable tips explain how to set rules, form bonds with the students, and create an equitable classroom atmosphere.

2. **Tony Nichols,** a kindergarten teacher in Richwood, West Virginia, explains how a circus-themed classroom can be the solution to classroom management woes. Easily adaptable to any theme, Tony's ideas can be used to guide students through daily routines, enhance their academic skills, and encourage good behavior.

3. **Ginger Mendenhall,** an elementary school instructor in Oklahoma, suggests a cheap and effective way to transition between activities in classrooms where transition times can take over instruction time. Use a dancing bear or a singing bunny to get students focused, on task, and ready to learn.

4. **KJ Bailey,** a second-grade teacher from Punta Gorda, Florida, involves students with their communities by asking them what they want to be when they grow up. Based on student answers, KJ invites community and family members into the classroom to share fun facts about their profession.

▧ 1. Building the Atmosphere

Elizabeth Grelle Kruse
Chicago, Illinois

Recommended Level: Grades K–3

Overall Objective: Start the school year right in your classroom. Through forming personal connections, observing students closely, and setting rules and enforcing them consistently, you can build an atmosphere conducive to learning.

The question of how an early-childhood or elementary teacher begins to manage a classroom can often go way beyond textbooks and college classes. Courses are often designed to teach the fundamentals and the educational backgrounds in order to prepare future teachers for teaching. Teachers are prepared with all the latest reading, writing, math, or science curriculum, but they are given little preparation for building the atmosphere for an effective learning environment. Teachers must be able to create a classroom community built out of respect, where students are safe both physically and emotionally. When it comes to learning how to manage different behaviors inside the classroom, you can't easily find the answers in your college child-development book. This is unfortunate because teachers need to learn how to make the classroom a community before actual teaching can begin. I will discuss what I believe to be the major factors in creating a well-managed classroom community in the early childhood years. I will address these factors separately, but they all complement each other. These factors include forming bonds, making observations, setting up guidelines, and being consistent.

Form Bonds

I believe there must be a bond created between the teacher and each of his or her students before "real" teaching can occur. I learned this early on as I observed my mother, a teacher, when she interacted with children, as well as my fourth- and fifth-grade teachers. All of these teachers created a nurturing learning environment.

In college, I was fortunate to student teach with another great teacher who practiced the belief I hold to be true: You must establish a personal connection with your students. Each day, she would talk to her students about her dog. She told them his name, Bobo, and started each day with personal stories about her dog mostly, but also about her husband or her own children. I watched as her students became more and more fascinated with the stories their teacher told. Even more important than the stories was the transformation of the children. They were spellbound by their teacher and gave her their complete attention. In return, the children wanted to be there, wanted to learn, and their behavior displayed that.

I begin each year by giving a part of myself to my students. I form connections with them by sharing simple events from my own life. I might talk to them about what I made for dinner last night before we begin our morning meeting. I might bring up something from the morning news or how my cat, Toonsie, woke me up by licking my nose. While I am sharing my stories, I am also watching to see who is smiling, who shakes his head, and what topics are of interest to whom. I then collect these observations, so I can learn more about each of my students.

The idea of sharing yourself with your students is simple, but I have found it to be very important. Often, children entering kindergarten are a little scared and not sure what their role is in the classroom. I can see my students opening up and becoming more comfortable with me and with our class from day one. My students then share their stories with me, form common interests with other children, and quickly begin making friendships. As a result, a sense of belonging and trust has been built on all levels in our classroom.

Observe

Children genuinely want to learn, they want to be in a safe place, and they tend to want to be where the other children are. In the early childhood years, before you begin teaching any subject, it is imperative to build the foundation of your classroom. So how do you do that? You must first start each year by doing a lot of observing. Don't be so quick to jump right into assessing students' prereading, writing, and math skills. Don't rush into teaching this semester's goals or worry about how the children need to recite the Pledge of Allegiance by next week. Wait about two weeks before you start teaching the first theme of the year. This is the time, the crucial time, for you to set the foundation of your classroom. It must be a priority! If you don't establish good classroom management early on, you are less likely to establish a classroom of well-behaved and engaged learners as the year continues.

Let the children explore the classroom. Your job now is to watch to see how developed your students are socially. Watch, with minimal interaction, to see how they respond to other children, how they share their toys, how they clean up, and so on. Take note of which children need help solving minor peer conflicts and which children seem to show an interest in playing with dolls. Spend a little time talking with each child individually to learn about him or her first as a unique child. This will enable you to be more effective when the time comes for instruction.

Set Rules

After you have observed for a while, it is time to use your observations to set the rules and expectations in your classroom. Get your students involved in the process of creating what can and cannot happen in your classroom. Give them the responsibility for what happens in the classroom, and involve them in the understanding of why rules are important. For example, if you observe students arguing over the blocks, use it as a problem-solving opportunity. "I noticed some children were taking blocks from other children's towers to use them for their own. What do you think we should do about that?" In my class, we made several rules from this one example. These included (1) only four children can be in the block area at a time, so there will be enough space and blocks for the children to build; (2) the children agreed that you cannot take blocks off other towers; and (3) if more blocks are needed, they have to talk to each other to work out a solution.

Making rules together gives my students power and ownership in the classroom. I could have put a sign in the block area with a number 4 on it and told the kids that only four children are allowed in there at a time. Instead, the children took ownership for the rule. As a result, a minicommunity was created.

Enforce Rules Consistently

Once your class has established classroom rules, they must be consistently enforced. If you decide that the children need to raise their hand to share comments and answers, you have to avoid responding to the child that yells out—the first time and the fiftieth time. If you call on students with their hands up mostly but still acknowledge the ones who don't, the rule is not going to work because you are not consistent. It will be challenging not to respond to the child that calls out. Ignore that child, and respond to those who are raising their hand by saying something like, "Oh, Jessica, I'm going to call on you because you are raising your hand." This will take time, but eventually, the children will understand what is expected of them and feel comfortable knowing this will always be the rule.

Communicate in Multiple Ways

I have found that my students don't want to listen to my voice every time I want to tell them something. Because of this, I teach my students what to do by using different techniques. For example, if I want to talk to my group in the middle of a center time and everyone is busy working, I simply turn off the lights. The children know to freeze when that happens. I could also clap my hands in a pattern. The children know to stop what they are doing and repeat my pattern. Try whispering to your students during group time when the children are getting a little noisy. You'll be surprised how quickly they will stop to hear what you are saying. Walk down the hallway with the kids blowing up their cheeks. They love it, but it also reminds them to quiet their voices when they are in the hall.

Each year, I incorporate sign language into my classroom. My students love to use it, and it provides me with a tool to communicate without distracting the children's learning while managing the class. For example, when I am teaching a lesson or reading a story to my class, a student needing to use the restroom does not need to interrupt to ask for permission. The student makes the "restroom" sign; I nod my head; the student leaves; and class continues without disruption. My students use sign language in other situations as well. A child might remind another child to sit down during a story by making the "sit" sign. Students often congratulate each other with a sign (good work, perfect, wow, etc.). I have found sign to be a wonderful instructional and innovative teaching tool while also providing the children with the foundation of a new language.

HelpfulTips

Just as each child has his or her own personality, each group of children will also have a unique personality. From class to class, the blending of personalities will make for a distinctive community of learners. If you take the time to form bonds with students, observe the chemistry and interactions within your classroom, set classroom guidelines accordingly as you confer with your students, and maintain consistency, you will be well on the road to a productive and enjoyable school year.

---

2. Creating a Thematic Classroom Environment

Tony Nichols
Richwood, West Virginia

Recommended Level: Grades K–3+

Overall Objective: Create a unique learning community for students, structured around a theme, and use the theme to establish classroom routines, opportunities for skill practice, and guidelines for behavior management.

Materials Needed:

- Large circus pictures or paper cutouts of ringmaster, lion tamer, elephants, lions, dancing bears, clown faces, popcorn kernels, admission tickets, stars

- Construction paper circles cut with an Ellison cutter
- Popcorn containers
- Graphing ring
- Pocket chart

- Bungee cord
- Circus cloth material
- Clothespins
- Circus animal foams

Each year, I create a unique classroom environment integrating a yearly theme to assist students with learning classroom routines, academic skills, and appropriate behavior. Even after they have graduated from my class, students will remember the things they did and the organization of the classroom. Recently, a student who is now a parent reminded me of the "Wheel of Fortune" spinner I used for behavior management in a third-grade classroom over 15 years ago. That spinner is still stored in my garage. Maybe it is time to pull it out again.

This year, I constructed a kindergarten classroom to resemble a circus. Next week, we'll take our culminating field trip to the city for the Ringling Bros. and Barnum & Bailey Circus. The following is the procedure I used to make the year a memorable one for these five- and six-year-olds.

Routines

Each morning, students entered the room with several "circus acts" to perform. First, they purchased a circus ticket to enter the classroom. The cost of the entry ticket varied throughout the year so students would quickly learn to identify coins. Students chose or counted the play money needed and placed it in the cash register where they received their entrance ticket. Tickets were then placed in a pocket chart to display morning attendance. Next, students graphed whether they were eating hot or cold lunch by placing paper popcorn kernel cutouts in popcorn containers labeled HOT or COLD. (I bought mine at the dollar bin at Target.) The containers were easy for students to count and tally the lunch count. I displayed the classroom helpers for the day in an area labeled Circus Stars. I used five large florescent paper stars and labeled each with the following jobs: line leader, morning message helper, calendar helper, clean up monitor, and lunch with teacher. Each student made a circus animal from a Foamies kit purchased from Michaels, an arts and crafts store. I labeled each animal with the students' names. The animals were hung alphabetically by the students' first names and pinned to each of the stars to announce the helpers for the day (I used clothespins to attach them). I rotated them each day. Students quickly learned the system and would not allow me to ever make a mistake or forget to change them.

Academic Skills

I purchased a bungee cord from a local teacher store and used it as a tightrope across the classroom. Even though it came in handy for hanging student work and wet art projects, I used mine to post letters and sounds. I posted the letter and picture cards from the reading basal to help students learn beginning sounds of words. The pictures were readily available and labeled to help students with sound sorts and writing activities.

Daily, students used an area on the wall where a lion tamer was posted. Students counted the number of animals the trainer had in a ring (I used a graphing ring hooked to the chalkboard with magnets). Students wrote the number on the chalkboard, practicing counting and number writing. After the semester, I used the lion tamer to count a set of ten and ones for teen-number practice. Students learned the months of the year and sets of numbers using an elephant parade set I purchased from a teacher store. Students built a yearly number line using plastic, multicolored, triangular festival flags I purchased from a party store. I hung them from the ceiling, and each day at calendar time, we posted the number of the day on each flag using an index card. Multiples of 5 and 10 were in blue, while the others were on yellow index cards. We practiced counting the flags daily.

I made dancing bears dressed in different costumes and labeled them with all the color words students needed to learn. I made mine from an old coloring book pattern.

I used a balloon poster to post students' birthdays. Children received helium balloons on special days, such as birthdays, and rewards for good work. Some were donated from the local florist.

I used circus material purchased at Wal-Mart for window treatments, calendars, and bulletin boards. I purchased a large clown from a teacher store to greet students outside the classroom door and one to record students' height and weight throughout the year. I hung a child-sized parachute in the book corner to represent a big top.

Behavior

We followed the motto, "Have a Circus Day!" I made clown faces for each child in the classroom and then laminated each one. I assigned one to each student by labeling the clowns with students' names. I did not include a mouth on the clowns but used a dry-erase marker to draw them. All students' clowns began the day with a smiling face. If a child misbehaved, their clown face was erased and changed to a straight face, indicating a warning. If the face was changed again to a frown face, students received corrective feedback to improve behavior. Students whose clown was still smiling at the end of the day received a construction paper smile made with an Ellison cutter, and my aide or parent volunteer drew the face on. We labeled the smiles with the following student information throughout the year to help students learn basic information about themselves: students' first, last, and middle names, addresses, phone numbers, birthdays, and lunch numbers.

To teach teamwork, well-behaved students with smiling clowns also received a marble to fill a popcorn container to earn the whole classroom a treat, such as popcorn or ice cream. Students with good behavior also placed their morning circus ticket in a container to be drawn for a door prize each day. Parents provided door prizes such as yo-yos for the letter *Y* or pencils for the letter *P*. I used this for an academic show and tell, as all the door prizes began with the letter sound we were currently studying.

HelpfulTips

The more commercial materials you can find at a teacher store, the less work you will need to complete yourself. After the year, package all the materials together so you can reuse it for another year. I like to rotate themes about every four to five years. I rarely do the same one year after year, keeping myself motivated and interested year to year. I try to think of themes the students will like and remember and could be adapted to other grades, should I transfer. Ideas can be used to increase skill level, such as a multiplication tightrope or a lion tamer demonstrating division facts for each day. The behavior management would work for several grade levels before becoming juvenile.

3. Transition Time

Ginger Mendenhall
Ponca City, Oklahoma

Recommended Level: Grades K–4

Overall Objective: Use nonverbal signals to streamline transition time and make it fun for students. This technique will increase classroom time for academic learning.

Materials Needed: Singing animal (many varieties are sold online or in stores during holiday seasons)

Turn those stressful transition times in your day into a fun experience for the students. Have you seen those singing hamsters, singing bunnies at Easter, dancing and singing gorillas on Valentine's Day? Get them! They make the best transition timer you can find. Students love the singing and dancing of the animal or character, and the teacher loves the shortened transition time.

Choose a different singing animal or character for each type of transition. This enables students to recognize the song and know what is expected without you saying a word. Times for use could include lining up, changing to a different subject, getting out supplies, moving to a learning area, and on and on.

Transition time does not have to cause a problem or take up your valuable learning time. Place the singing animal or character where the students can see it and squeeze it, and watch them dance as they follow the prescribed procedure. Reducing the difficulty of transition time will create more instructional time in your day. Students will also enjoy the fun and often dance as they line up or put things away.

HelpfulTips

Because you make several transitions during the day, get a different animal or character to match the designated procedure. An example would be the dog that sings "Don't Worry, Be Happy" to line up to go home for the day. Another example would be the bunny that sings "Yummy, Yummy, Yummy, I Got Love in My Tummy" to go to lunch. This helps students associate the song with the desired action or behavior.

Have fun! Get creative! The students will love it!

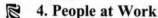 **4. People at Work**

KJ Bailey
Punta Gorda, Florida

Recommended Level: Grades 1–4

Overall Objective: Involve family members and people from the community in your students' classroom learning, using this unit on different professions.

Standards Met (Florida):

English Language Arts: Selects materials to read for pleasure; Reads for information to use in performing a task and learning a new task; Uses simple materials of the reference system to obtain information

Materials Needed:

- Paper, pencils, crayons
- Books and encyclopedias
- Parent letter
- Computers
- Parent and community volunteers

In my second-grade class, we begin by discussing the jobs of the world and their duties. As jobs are being named I write them on the board along with two or three of their associated duties. Now that I have their little minds rolling, I ask them about what they want to be when they grow up. Once this is accomplished, we begin a rough draft of a short writing piece on their job of choice. The drafts are collected, checked, and returned within a day. When the students have revised the piece and are ready with a final draft, they receive a small dye-cut of a person. These dye-cut people represent themselves, and they are able to dress their person to match their profession. I have all of my students present their final copies to the class and answer any questions that their classmates might have for them.

Once the papers are turned in, I send a letter home to the families and out to the community for "Community Reader" volunteers. I always try to find people with jobs that my students have chosen to come in for this. All of the readers are asked to either bring in their favorite book or choose one from our classroom library. They are also asked to talk about their particular job, things that they might do on a daily basis, and why it is important to continue reading. I have had many people come to my class to participate in this fun-filled unit. I have had a firefighter who let the students try on his gear, a newscaster with his camera operator who let them do a mock news program, a K9 deputy and his dogs who put on a show, and a scrub tech from a local hospital, to name a few. Once the readers are finished reading and discussing what it is that they do, there are always questions, lots of questions. After all, these students are seven- and eight-year-olds! But I think this unit could be accomplished with first graders and adapted to remain interesting for third and fourth graders.

After the readers have left our room, we begin to make our foldables (the students usually make them big enough to have six to eight readers on each foldable). These foldables consist of the reader's name, profession, duties they talked about, and two reasons they gave to the class to keep reading. To show our appreciation to each reader for taking the time to come in and share with us, we always make and send thank-you letters.

Helpful Tips

- Have a variety of job books for the students to look at and read prior to the unit.
- When introducing this unit, take note of what the students want to be. As much as possible, try to get people with these jobs to be your readers.
- Send parent letters home early, and remind them of this fun unit often.
- Make sure you not only get families involved but the community as well.
- Keep a calendar of all the scheduled readers and their times.
- Always call in advance to confirm your reader is coming.
- Always remember to have fun, and keep reading!

Differentiating Instruction in Regular and Inclusive Classrooms

Overview, Chapters 5–9

5. **Kendra Jiles,** a K–5 self-contained teacher from Georgetown, South Carolina, describes how to organize a special education class for students of varying abilities. Her class opening routines and method of teaching the calendar and the weather will help every class run more smoothly.

6. **Ginger Mendenhall,** an elementary school teacher from Oklahoma, differentiates learning across the curriculum, making lessons adaptable for students of all ability levels. This activity board engages students' four learning modalities through auditory, visual, tactile, and kinesthetic activities.

7. **Sharla Steever,** a third-grade teacher from Hill City, South Dakota, borrows from the IEP model used in special education to help her keep track of her general education students. Her Personal Education Plan (PEP) Books are individually designed for each student, recognizing their personal learning needs.

8. **Brandy Bailey,** a fourth-grade language arts teacher in Mississippi, uses reader's and writer's workshops and learning centers to differentiate

learning in a safe, judgment-free environment. All of Brandy's students are held to high standards regardless of ability in her inclusion classroom.

9. **Kelli Higgins,** a third-grade teacher from East Peoria, Illinois, has students roll story cubes to select reading response activities tailored to different learning styles. When Kelli takes her story cubes out of the closet, "the kids get excited."

▨ 5. Considering Special Education

Creative Scheduling, Classroom Management, and Inclusion

Kendra Jiles
Georgetown, South Carolina

Recommended Level: Grades K–3

Overall Objective: To have students collect and analyze data, and answer questions about the data. Students will also apply number sense and problem-solving skills in relation to functional concepts, such as the calendar and weather.

The needs, the wants, the goals, the standards . . . These topics and more confront teachers who teach special needs as they consider how to set up their classroom for optimal learning experiences, how to get the most out of their day, and how to ensure effective time and classroom management.

As a special education teacher, you serve as the case manager for your students. When planning the schedule for the year, everything has to be timed. This allows for smooth transitions from mainstream classes back to your classroom without major disruption. For those students who need additional support, special education teachers must work closely with content-area teachers to modify assignments and provide the physical support that is needed within that mainstream setting. Teaching special education is a joy, but one must be able to structure the classroom to allow multilevel and multiage students to have lasting experiences.

The day begins with *circle time*. This is the first activity of the day, where students get to come together, building a sense of community within the classroom. During this time, several standards are covered. Concepts and topics covered relate to weather, temperature, seasons, days of the week, months of the year, the date, reading functional words, bar graphs, subtraction, place value, numbers, number patterns, time, problem solving, and so on. Students assemble in two semicircular lines on the floor. The younger students are in the front, and the older students are in the back.

Circle time begins with the students writing the date and reciting the days of the week and then the months of the year. For older students, who may become bored or feel that saying those things are for little kids, have them recite in a foreign language, such as Spanish. From there, a discussion is held pertaining to what the current day of the week is, what the previous day was, and what the next day will be. Weather is then discussed. For those students who do not dress properly, this becomes a time where they can go to the board and draw a picture of a child wearing appropriate attire. How the sky looks is also discussed. This is turned into a form of data collection. Students write or draw pictures of each day's weather and use it to answer questions at the end of the week.

Next, students count by ones, twos, fives, and so on. This encourages the learning of multiplication facts as well as patterns. Discussion is then held about which two numbers the day's temperature is between. A chosen student plots the number on a thermometer. Data is collected daily on these temperatures to help analyze patterns and to plot increases and decreases. The calendar is the focus for the next part of the discussion. Students answer comprehension questions pertaining to holidays or other special events and what those days mean. Other questions pertain to the number of days in the month and the number of specific days (How many Saturdays are in this month?). In addition, language arts is incorporated to remind students which words should be capitalized. The lunch menu is also read. This expands the discussion into the different food groups, which things are healthy, and how to recognize words in restaurants when they are traveling with their parents.

Place value is also discussed. Each day, students add a straw to a holder to show the number of days they have been in school. Students begin their knowledge of base ten. In addition, students who are subtracting have to subtract the number of days they have been in school from the number of days in the school year to find out the number of days left. Other topics discussed during this time relate to behavioral expectations and to motor skills, such as tying shoes. Students also are reminded of their daily classroom duties to help everyone take a part in the classroom. Then it's time for read aloud.

HelpfulTips

- Find science and social studies teachers who are willing to work with your students.
- Find special-area time slots to insert your students into other classrooms that are accepting of differences.
- Within the schedule, create times for students to receive individual instruction.
- For whole-group activities, have a list of questions geared to the developmental and instructional level of all the children.

---

6. Mix and Match

Ginger Mendenhall
Ponca City, Oklahoma

Recommended Level: Grades K–5+, including special needs and gifted students

Overall Objective: The overall objective of the Mix and Match Board is to master the content of the desired subject matter in a way that will help all learners be successful and give students choice in their learning process. Teachers may also allow students to choose the activity that matches their learning preference; the teacher may also require the students to complete one activity that is not in their preferred learning category. This strengthens other learning preferences to allow students greater success with varied teachers' teaching styles in the future.

Materials Needed: Materials will match the activities placed in the Mix and Match Board.

This activity board is designed to reach the various learning styles of all the students. The board includes auditory, visual, tactile, and kinesthetic activities. The board also gives choices for students to build on their strengths and to begin to develop skills within their weaker learning preferences.

Four Learning Modalities

Auditory Activities	Visual Activities
Make auditory tape	Draw a picture
Have a discussion with classmate	Make a poster
Write a play and perform	Flash cards
Write a poem and perform	Make a quilt poster
Write and perform a radio announcement	Mural
Musical performance	Summarize and illustrate
Panel discussion	Coloring or flip book
Court trial	Costume
Debate	Timeline
Quiz show	Collage
Tactile Activities	**Kinesthetic Activities**
Felt story board	Floor game
Drawing	Role play/acting
Diorama	Pantomime
Clay	Jump rope while answering
Manipulatives	Conduct a survey
Puzzle	Build a machine
Make model	Interview
Character paper dolls	Puppet show
Scrapbook	Campaign for a belief
Graph	Develop a product
Tapestry or quilt	Demonstration

Note: More activities can be found on the Internet.

The previous page includes activities for the four learning modalities. The Mix and Match game board (see example at the end of this chapter) is used for any content area, reading, language arts, math, science, social studies, and others. Each square needs to be filled in with an activity that corresponds to the teacher's desired content. The squares also need to include varied activities from each list for the different learning style preferences. The students and the teacher may decide together, or the teacher may make a prior decision about how many squares each student needs to complete. The students may make a diagonal or straight three-in-a-row (like bingo) pattern for completion of the assignment. The teacher may require students to complete one from their learning style preference and one from a learning style weakness.

This Mix and Match Board is also a wonderful tool to adapt for students with learning challenges. You can assign three squares to some students while, at the same time, assigning only one or two squares to another. For the gifted students, you may assign the entire Mix and Match Board.

The Mix and Match Board can be created in Excel. Select nine cells and copy and paste to a Microsoft Word document. Fill in the squares for the assignment desired. Be sure to vary the activities to cover each student's learning style preference. It is also a good idea to have a time frame agreed upon before beginning the Mix and Match Board, so students can be aware of time constraints and be successful in a timely completion.

The following is a sample Mix and Match Board for reading.

MIX and MATCH: Read a book about animals approved by your teacher. Choose at least three activities.

Make a list of the animals in your book. Use some resource materials to research your animals. Make a book with at least 10 pictures of the animals. Write three interesting	With some of your classmates, create index cards of the animals and index cards with a description or fact about each animal. Place all cards face down on the floor	Create your own activity.

facts for each of the animals that you chose. (V/T)	and play a game of Concentration, matching the animal card with the description/fact card. (V/T/K)	
Act out 10 animals, including their distinguishing movements and sounds. Perform for the class and let them guess the name of the animal. (A/V/K)	Write a story about your favorite animal in your book, and tell why you would like to have that kind of animal as your pet. Illustrate the story. (V/T)	Make an audiotape to name 10 animals. When you name an animal, tell one important fact about it. Be creative with your voice. Have fun! (A)
Write an alliteration using the names of 10 animals. Make your sentences funny. Read the sentences to two of your classmates. (A/V/T)	Ask a friend to be your partner. Put the names of the animals on index cards. While your friend holds up the card, you will spell the animal's name and jump rope while you are spelling. (A/V/T/K)	Find another book about animals. Make a comparison chart (T-chart or Venn diagram) to illustrate the animals' similarities and differences. (V/T)

7. Personal Education Plan (PEP) Books

Sharla Steever
Hill City, South Dakota

Recommended Level: Grades K–5+

Overall Objective: To become a diagnostic teacher, able to efficiently track students' progress and identify their learning difficulties. Your students will take charge of their own learning, and receive a tailor-made education, using the "Reading by Myself" and "Math by Myself" sections of their books.

Materials Needed:

- Three-ring binders, section dividers, labels
- Resources to copy

Over the years, my ideas about how I impact the learning of my students have changed. As a new teacher, I felt that my most important job was to deliver content to my students. Although this is still a vital piece of my job, I began to realize that lots of variables affect my students' ability to receive that content. The home life, interest areas, learning modes, and ability level of each student are just a few of the factors I began to evaluate. Although some of the factors, such as home life and backgrounds, are out of my control, many of the other factors are within my ability to affect. I decided that I needed to make the most of the areas I had the ability to change. It became apparent to me that, because each student learns in different ways, I needed to modify the methods I was using to deliver content. Over the past three to four years, I have become a much more diagnostic teacher. I spend a great deal of time as each year begins testing my students to find out where their strengths and weaknesses lie. I use computerized testing programs such as STAR Reading and Math, our state DAC's (Dakota Assessment Content Standards) standards assessment program, and our state's Achievement Series. I also use some one-on-one assessments to check for word decoding abilities, basic math skills, and reading skills. I use all of these assessments in September and combinations of them in December/January and March/April. I then track the data from the tests to guide my instruction.

I have developed a program I use in my classroom to promote the greatest level of academic growth in my students I can facilitate. I call the plan a PEP (Personal Education Plan) Book and it consists of a three-ring binder full of differentiated reading and math lessons. After compiling my test data, I look for areas of weakness. I put a plan together for each student that addresses those weaknesses. I use large-group instruction for a day or two to introduce concepts to my class, but then I follow up with small-group instruction in both reading and math. Students work in their PEP Books on their "Reading by Myself" or "Math by Myself" sections when they are not working with me. I call back small groups of three to five students at a time to work with me on learning objectives specific to their ability levels. My reading and math blocks consist of time for new instruction in small groups with me, time for practice on their own of concepts we have already covered, computer practice, accelerated reading time, and accelerated math quizzes.

The flow of an average reading or math time that is not a day of large-group instruction is as follows. I ask my students to get their PEP Books from the shelf. They take them to their desks and begin working on their "Reading by Myself" or "Math by Myself" sections of their books. These sections have materials in them that are specific to the individual student. The work is at an independent level, so not much instruction is needed from me, and it is designed to strengthen skills rather than introduce new skills. While students are working independently, I pull small groups out to work on new concepts with me. Groups of three to five students sit with me at my table, and we work on reading and math skills specific to the levels of the groups. During these blocks of time, students have control over when they do each part of their independent work as long as they finish all parts in the given time. They can take a break from their PEP Books and work on the computer for a while if one is open. (I have either reading or math programs loaded and ready for each class period.) They can also read silently in accelerated reading books and take quizzes during this time. I have found that the responsibility put on my students to take charge of their own learning has made them independent learners, and I have almost no behavior issues during these times. As I finish my small-group instruction time, I take the last few minutes to check in with each student to see if they completed the tasks assigned for that time.

Expectations are actually a very important piece of this program. The first time I used it, I spent a full week not really doing much new instruction but overseeing the flow of my room to make sure students understood what I expected them to do. I helped them develop the flow of moving from one thing to the next on their schedules, and I also worked with them to learn how to ask each other for help before coming to me. By taking the time to instill my expectations, I avoided having a lot of interruptions in my small-group instruction time.

The greatest benefit of this program in my classroom is that my students are receiving a tailor-made education, which allows them to progress at their own pace. Since I have begun this program in my classroom, student growth has increased tremendously. My average increase is 1.7 years in reading and 1.5 years in math between the months of September and March. I have had students make as much as a three-year jump in their ability levels by using this program. It provides for the needs of my lowest ability-level groups to my highest, and it also ensures equity of my time with each student. The other benefit to this program is that after a time, if I have students that still have not moved ahead, I have a great deal of data to share with parents and our special education teacher if academic testing is needed.

Now after using this program for a while, I have a great deal of resources ready to go for most any problem area a new student might have. I have taken the resources I have collected and put them into large binders. At the beginning of the year or when I receive a new student, my resources are ready to plug into a plan that will get them going at a level and pace specific to each need. Although there is a great deal of work involved in starting up this program, the benefits far outweigh the work. When I did my first set of testing after initiating this program in my classroom, I saw an average gain of eight months in the first two months' time. It was one of the most thrilling moments of my teaching career. Watching my students grow and succeed in their learning is a benefit I get to have each day. It has transformed me as a teacher, and I can't wait to continue to find new and even better ways of meeting my students' needs.

Helpful Tips

The one thing that this program does create is a lot of different kinds of correcting. It is helpful to have someone, such as a student aid or paraprofessional, to help you with the correcting; however, I have done it alone as well. I create a schedule for each student to check off the things they have accomplished that day, and once all items are finished, they put a sticker on their charts. I can look at a glance to see if everyone has completed their reading and math each day.

8. Learning to Teach Inclusion

Brandy Bailey
Hernando, Mississippi

Recommended Level: Grades K–5+

Overall Objective: To create a classroom that meets all educational needs for a wide range of students by organizing and using learning centers efficiently and effectively to differentiate learning.

I use differentiated learning to teach in my fourth-grade language arts inclusion classroom. My students' abilities range from preprimer to sixth grade. I have used centers I created and bought to differentiate their class work. I also use modifications and workshop methods.

Who are we trying to reach with differentiated learning? In my classroom, I begin each year with a story about a very special child. The book is *Crow Boy* by Taro Yashima (1955). Although the book was written in 1955, it delivers a powerful message for today. The main character, Chibi, was not able to learn in school. His classmates were unable to look past his odd behaviors and see the talents he possessed. They taunted and ridiculed him until a special teacher opened their eyes. With the new teacher's help, they came to see Chibi as someone special. This book helps my students learn to look for strengths instead of focusing on the weaknesses of their classmates.

What does this book say to me as a teacher? To me, it gives a purpose and a challenge. I must strive to meet the needs of every student in my classroom. Can I reach every child? I like to think yes. Does meeting needs ensure that all children will perform on grade level? No. I provide the opportunities for learning and consistently push my students to do their best. If I do this, I feel I have done my part. I expect each child to play a part in his or her education also. Some students will always be high performers, but some struggle to make it out of high school. Just like Chibi, both kinds of students can be successful in their own time and their own way.

I have been an inclusion teacher for five years. During this time, I have seen all sorts of students thrive in an inclusive environment. Teaching inclusion students can be quite a daunting task. I must provide for students with ADD, emotional issues, physical limitations, and learning disabilities in the same classroom as gifted and regular education students. To meet the needs of such a diverse group, I am required to merge learning styles, multiple intelligences, and disabilities in unique manners. I use many forms of differentiated instruction to meet my students' needs, including leveling, grouping, and modification of work.

How do I use workshops to differentiate learning? I found that readers' and writers' workshops, as a teaching design, are the most effective ways to accomplish this for me. The student-centered approach of these workshops helps all students feel successful and encourages higher-order thinking skills. Before I began to use readers' and writers' workshops, I found an immense amount of research online from teachers who use workshops and are willing to share their great ideas. Of the ideas I researched, I found that using learning centers instead of work-sheets was what worked for me. It has given me the freedom to put a major focus on scaffolding my teaching. I am now able to spend time focusing on the needs of those students who are lacking important prerequisites for fourth grade.

Let me take you through a typical language arts block in my class-room. Please understand that fire drills, assemblies, student behavior, or administrative procedures will pop up. Just go with the flow, and know that if you don't get to something today, it's okay. In a center classroom, there is always tomorrow.

You always need to have an introduction. Read a book, make a chart, play a quick game, use a PowerPoint, or discuss a focus skill. I try to spend only 10 minutes here. I give directions for a group activity, skill sheet, or independent project. Then students head into the work period.

During our work period, we complete our assignment for the day, work in centers, complete contract work, or research current topics on much higher levels. There are two strands of thought on the subject of leveling when in small groups. One insists on having groups with all ability levels represented. Another allows for leveling. I tend to level. I have found that while students benefit from being with different ability levels, my lower-level ones tended to sit back and let the higher-level students do all the work. I usually level when grading an activity or doing a project. I use varying ability levels when introducing a new subject, peer reading, or nongraded projects. I feel this compromise helps my students learn the best. When producing group work, I often give a different colored marker for each student to write with. I can quickly see who did all the work, and no one needs to "snitch" on a group member. Partner reading and teacher conferences are completed here also. Conferences are very important. Whether in a small group or one on one, close contact with your students is a determining factor in student achievement.

We end with a sharing time. As a large group, the class holds a discussion about what we learned today. We read from our current literature selection, read our own writing, or review our objectives for the week.

How do I use centers to differentiate learning? I have been using centers for many years and have developed the following four tips to use centers more effectively.

1. Define goals for each child. Centers are fun, and can be educational, if they can be assessed. When I began using centers, my first mistake was to allow center days without defined goals. I allowed students to play games and work projects for the purpose of "educational fun." Big mistake! They jumped from center to center without learning anything. Oh sure, they could tell you they worked on fact and opinion, but where was the proof? How could I keep track of the skills they needed to work on? To fix this problem, I created a chart to list strengths and weaknesses for each student. Students could then see the areas they needed to work on. I based these on the previous year's MCT (Mississippi Curriculum Test 2) results. I add other skills as needed, based on weekly assessments. The students have defined goals. They know what they need to work on and get to choose when they work on it. Choosing the activity to complete puts them in charge of their own learning. By keeping children an active partner in their education, I am showing them that I have faith in their choices. I believe they are capable of making decisions that will impact their future.

2. Write and enforce class rules. Off-task behaviors are always a problem in a center program. Have a plan of action for these behaviors. I have an alternative activity for those students. Worksheets! If students can't participate in the center activities, they complete many worksheets on the current topic of study. This usually jogs half of them into working. The others can be pulled into a small group to complete the worksheets with the teacher. Just remember that life is not like TV. Your students do not come from homes like yours. They may not have the social skills needed for center work, or they may have any number of emotional issues. Find what motivates them, and make it a point to love your kids. When students in my class has to move to worksheets, they also spend time walking at recess. This gives them time to reflect on their misdeed and get energy out at the same time. If all else fails, conference with the parents. Explain the rules and address the issue. Using a grading rubric for your centers will help you in this regard. Parents are more likely to act when grades are involved.

3. Create a plan for organizing centers. Organizing class time spent on center work and placement of centers are the subject of many books. The following methods have all worked well for me.

Method One: When just starting out with centers, many teachers make a few centers for each topic of study and use them to cover that topic. You select the centers used by students. Centers are used a set number of times a week, and whole- or small-group activities compose the rest of the week's instruction. Teachers are able to build their centers as they progress through the year. A weekly assessment is given based on the center activities and whole-group instruction. The data can be used to assign new centers.

Method Two: Centers are placed in buckets. Teachers give students a choice of centers based on the current topic of study. Centers can be completed as a small group, partner group, or individually. Centers are used at a set time each day, and students rotate through each center by the end of the week. A weekly assessment is given based on the center activities and whole-group instruction. The assessment data can be used to assign new centers.

Method Three: Centers are labeled in bins around the room. Centers are chosen by the students and teacher based on the child's needs at the current time and topic of study. Students use contracts or checklists to keep track of their needs and the teacher's requirements. Whole-group instruction is limited, and small-group instruction is maximized. A weekly assessment is given based on the center activities and small-group instruction. The data can be used to assign new centers.

4. Be flexible. At the beginning of the year, I have to gauge my students. I use pretests to determine my students' needs. Second, I judge their temperament as a group. With some classes, I have been able to remove all desks from my room and let them sit on the floor to work. With others, I have had to have a more firm hold. If you are flexible in your planning, you will work well with all three methods. If you tend to have issues with flexibility, start small. As you see things starting to work well, everything will be easier to handle.

What do I expect from my students when I differentiate their learning? All students are held to high standards in my classroom. We may have different standards based on ability, or we may use different ways of proving mastery of our skills. My students know that I want them to reach further than they have before. I encourage, push, reward, and in the end, celebrate with each one. By teaching in an inclusion classroom, I have found that all children have the ability to learn. By teaching with differentiated methods, I can see evidence of that learning. We may not master our skills at the same time, but all students can experience success. I have high expectations for my students, and their progress continues to astound me.

Reference

Yashima, T. (1955). *Crow boy.* New York: Viking Press.

9. Differentiation Using Story Cubes

Kelli Higgins
East Peoria, Illinois

Recommended Level: Grades 2–5

Overall Objective: To help students review a variety of story elements in ways that are interesting to them, use different intelligences, and meet their individual needs.

Materials Needed: The materials will depend on the activities you choose to include on your cube. A sample cube is printed at the end of this chapter, which you can copy and use as is or adapt to your specific lessons. All that is needed for the activities I've chosen are easily created handouts showing a rough outline of a T-shirt; a Venn diagram; a set of boxes to fill in, cut out, and make into a timeline chain; and graph paper with large squares.

When I take my story cubes out of the closet, the kids get excited. They know that it's not going to be more of the same old worksheets that go along with our reading series. They enjoy rolling the cube and reading what their assignment is. I allow them to roll the cube until they find an assignment they can really get excited about. Faster-working students may finish several different assignments from the cube in one class period, while others may just complete one activity. I find it is easy to keep a watchful eye over all of the projects; I can even work with a small group of students at a side table if I need to. When designing my cubes, I try to incorporate different areas of multiple intelligences. To use the cube in your class, print it out on cardstock.

The timeline chain is a linguistic and body or kinesthetic activity in which students write down six to eight main events from the story on 1" × 12" strips of paper. They arrange the sentence strips in order, then connect them loop-through-loop as a paper chain. The T-shirt design is an interpersonal and spatial project. Students are to reflect on the main character of the story and design a T-shirt that they might wear. The comic strip highlights the spatial and linguistic intelligences. Students are asked to retell the main story in a short and funny way. They need to draw simple, clear pictures, and write text and speech. The Venn diagram is intrapersonal and linguistic. Students compare and contrast the main character in the story to themselves. Making a dictionary is a linguistic activity. Students select 10 new or interesting words from the story. They arrange them in alphabetical order and look up their definitions in a real dictionary. The survey project is logical, mathematical, and linguistic. Students write a survey question that is somehow related to the story. They ask their classmates to vote on their choices. They collect data and record the results. Students then make a graph with the data.

Having a variety of projects to choose from makes these cubes a fun way to review a story.

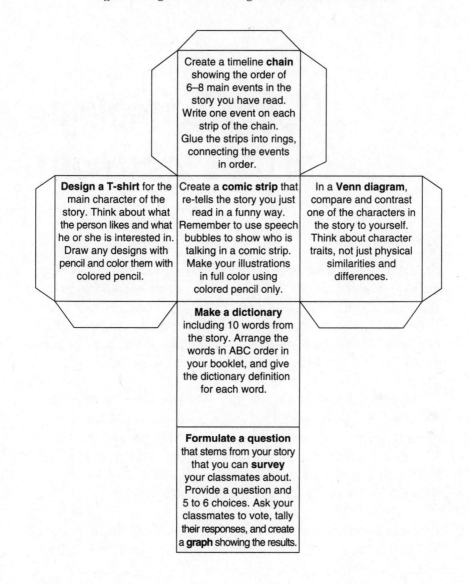

Create a timeline **chain** showing the order of 6–8 main events in the story you have read. Write one event on each strip of the chain. Glue the strips into rings, connecting the events in order.

Design a T-shirt for the main character of the story. Think about what the person likes and what he or she is interested in. Draw any designs with pencil and color them with colored pencil.

Create a **comic strip** that re-tells the story you just read in a funny way. Remember to use speech bubbles to show who is talking in a comic strip. Make your illustrations in full color using colored pencil only.

In a **Venn diagram**, compare and contrast one of the characters in the story to yourself. Think about character traits, not just physical similarities and differences.

Make a dictionary including 10 words from the story. Arrange the words in ABC order in your booklet, and give the dictionary definition for each word.

Formulate a question that stems from your story that you can **survey** your classmates about. Provide a question and 5 to 6 choices. Ask your classmates to vote, tally their responses, and create a **graph** showing the results.

Using Technology in the Classroom

Overview, Chapters 10–13

10. **Helen Melvin,** a retired second-grade teacher from Fort Kent, Maine, shares some useful tips on acquiring technology so teachers can have a varied and more interesting classroom. Helen suggests creating a slideshow of the class for families to enjoy, and she recommends participating in a worldwide social studies project. She also explains how to apply for grant money so that every classroom can afford to incorporate technology.

11. **Marianne Morin,** a reading and math teacher in Watkins Glen, New York, brings out the future author in her third- and fourth-grade students by having them read their work in front of an audience, using a karaoke machine. The class also writes and films their own skits based on historical events, uses WebQuests, and films a mock news show to enhance their learning through technology.

12. **LeAnn Morris,** the technology teacher at Empire Elementary in Nevada, teaches Internet-aided research to her fifth-grade class. Students research a technological invention, create a PowerPoint slideshow, and get to show off their accomplishments for their classmates and families.

13. **Michael Flynn,** a second-grade teacher from Massachusetts, hosts a bimonthly television show with his students, which the students write, plan, and film. His students get a chance to solidify the information they learned during the unit of study by putting it on film, and they have fun in the process.

☙ 10. Technology for a Varied and More Interesting Classroom

Helen Melvin
Fort Kent, Maine

Recommended Level: Grades K–5+

Overall Objective: To harness the many powerful advantages of incorporating technology into the curriculum and make learning more exciting and relevant for students. Learn about an Internet geology project and how to apply for technology grants.

Materials Needed: Computers with Internet access and any other technology

Students are like our school budgets: each year they are entirely different and require creative fine-tuning to get the most out of them. Gardner's theory on multiple intelligences has helped teachers add variety to their teaching methods and approaches. Many teachers now strive to make their lessons more relevant by offering hands-on experiences to get students excited about learning. It is so much easier to enhance the learning process without having to be tied strictly to textbooks, whiteboard, and paper. It is very important to add variety in the classroom to reach today's students.

Technology today is compatible with many styles of teaching and learning. Our school's purchasing of computers in the early 1990s opened new doors for me as a teacher. It also provided new learning tools for my students. The use of technology, in its various packages, has not only benefited me, but my students now have the potential to reach higher levels of learning and learn in a multitude of ways. Students can use computers in the classroom to read articles or books online, to research topics, to collect and graph weather information, to create maps and graphs, and to compare themselves with students from around the world. The technology doesn't need to be expensive or require training to have a positive impact on the way students learn. Students have improved attitudes, improved achievement, and strive for higher test scores. They are more engaged in their learning and show new enthusiasm for learning. A computer does not shame them when they get a wrong answer—it is less intimidating. Reinforcement of skills throughout the school year makes for improved retention. Technology does in a fun way what teachers tried to do in the past with papers of repeated skill work.

A great Internet geography/cultural project is the Flat Stanley Project. This project tracks Flat Stanley cutout dolls as they are mailed all over the world. Our class read the book *Flat Stanley* by Jeff Brown (1996) and then decided to join the official Flat Stanley Project (www.flatstanley.com). Students wrote to and mailed their Flat Stanley characters to locations around the globe. When their Flat Stanley characters came back to them, they read about their Flat Stanley characters' adventures and experiences; they saw pictures of the places their Flat Stanley characters visited and read stories created by other children concerning Stanley's experiences while in that country or state. The excitement in class was very contagious. Other classes wanted to know what was going on as we plotted and marked our large map in the hall. We also hosted Flat Stanley characters from other project locations. The visit by these cutouts from varied locations allowed my students to plan their activities together, take photo shoots, and write stories as we entertained each of these visitors for a week or more. This project would also be a great schoolwide activity.

Computers are an easy link with parents. There are many Web-hosting sites available to educators (scholastic.com, quia.com, schoolnotes.com, etc.). You can post the day's homework, coming events, special notices, and also add hyperlinks to topics or games that reinforce skills. Most parents like to know their child's homework for the day.

I also put together photo slideshows of all the special classroom activities. Most pictures have captions explaining the event. Parents view their first slideshow while waiting for their turn (sitting in the hallway) to meet with me during parent-teacher conferences in the fall. I put my laptop computer on a rolling cart in the hall and leave it near their chairs. Most parents go back to view the rest of the slideshow after their conference with me. Later that week, I mail them the slideshow so they have a copy. Parents are very pleased with the slideshow communication, as it keeps them abreast of all class activities.

I have never been bored as a teacher, even after 37 years. The best thing that has happened to schools is the large variety of technology available today one can use to enhance lessons. For the teacher who lacks resources, grants are plentiful on the Internet. A teacher can also look into fund raising (if permitted by your school). One should first consider discussing your classroom needs with your principal. If the school cannot help you financially, consider asking parents for old technology. One year, I asked parents for discarded technology toys (i.e., items that their children had outgrown). I obtained a number of LeapPads, Little Professors, Leapster Learning, and skill toys from parents who were happy to see them being used.

Besides computers, my classroom was home to old cassette players, used discarded book and tape sets, an old record player (I had educational records that still added variety to specific lessons), and many items that other teachers were no longer using (materials for varied ability levels). This past year, one student looked at a 33rpm record (never having seen one before) and said, "Miss, I'll bet you got this nice new disk with a grant! Wow! This disk is really neat!" One can find education in many places and sometimes by surprise.

When I began applying for grants, I searched for grants that would allow the purchase of technology hardware for my classroom. My first purchase was a good, working computer, which I could use to track students and plan my lessons. I also took in older models and upgraded them using funds from my grants. I then purchased printers (a color jet printer for pictures and a laser jet printer with copying capabilities), a scanner, digital cameras for student use, and two computer microscopes. As I continued applying for grants, I bought educational programs and games that would enhance my lessons; a large screen TV, which students could use to present their PowerPoints; a VCR to play great (discarded) educational programs on rocks, electricity, dinosaurs, and other topics; a CD/DVD player with surround sound; and an electronic *Jeopardy* game that allowed me to review skills and topics that are slowly forgotten when not reinforced during the year. The possibilities for adding to a classroom are endless and bounded only by imagination.

Grants are truly lifesavers when it comes to funding a classroom. Though I felt very insecure when writing my first grant, with time, they became less threatening. Don't be afraid to seek administrative help (most school districts welcome the extra money and tools for their district). Solicit ideas, assistance, and review criteria with your peers. It's fun to work cooperatively for the benefit of all.

Grant monies changed my teaching and also changed me as a teacher. Having extra technology for your students means that you can do fun activities that other teachers can only dream of. Your students will love school because it's never boring. Their enthusiasm also rubs off on you.

Helpful Tips

- Ask your principal or administrators if they know of available grants. That way, if they come across some grants and know you're interested, they'll pass the information on to you.
- Look on the Internet for available grants. There's usually a pretty good variety at the beginning of the school year, but there are grants given year round.
- If you want more than just a few hundred dollars, you may want to involve a colleague and complete a joint project. Many times, the monies increase when more than one classroom is involved.
- Don't be afraid to ask for help if you're not sure of the grant questions or the wording.
- Check each grant's rubric for accepting and approving grants. Make sure you've met all their criteria before sending in your application.
- Have an administrator or experienced grant-writing person go over your grant when you have finished completing the application.
- Keep your administration posted on your grant applications. It's important to have administrative support.

Reference

Brown, J. (1996). *Flat Stanley*. New York: HarperTrophy.

▧ 11. Incorporating Technology Into the Reading and Writing Curriculum

Marianne Morin
Watkins Glen, New York

Recommended Level: Grades 3–4

Overall Objective: To help students to use a variety of technology to discover, research, create, make decisions, work collaboratively in groups, organize thoughts, and share their newfound wisdom with others.

At the turn of the century, my principal told me she was changing my position at school. I was to move away from teaching first- and second-grade reading and move up to a new job with a new goal. She called it integrating technology into the third- and fourth-grade reading and writing curriculum. It was a very avant-garde move, and it came with no directions or training. Yikes!

There are two lines of thought as to the meaning of *incorporating technology into curriculum.* Some say it's the teacher who uses the technology as a teaching tool, using a computer or overhead to demonstrate examples, type out lesson plans, produce materials or slide shows, or even watching various educational TV shows, videos, or Internet sites as a way to build background knowledge or culminate a great unit. (Multiple-choice drill-and-skill practice would come under this category.)

Others think of technology integration as a way for students to share what they have learned, do research on the Internet, or to create and express their own ideas in a new and exciting way. According to this line of thought, students harness technology and use it to demonstrate what they know and can do. Technology is not a separate piece or unit of learning. It exists for students to access, use, organize, and disseminate information.

In the first definition, students take a passive role, and the teacher is the technology user. Occasionally a student can come up and circle something or put an X on the correct answer. Mostly, they sit at their desks and listen to the teacher or machine impart information. In the second definition, the students take an active role, and the teacher becomes the helper. Students discover, research, create, make decisions, work collaboratively in groups, organize thoughts, and share their new-found wisdom with others.

We started out with two carts filled with e-Mates. I just love these lightweight laptops because they brought computers to the desks of students. The children could type a story and insert a hand-drawn illustration into their own text. They also learned how to print out the finished product, change fonts, edit and revise, and spell check. One hundred third-grade students were able to complete projects without complaining. The work had become fun.

The next great technology we used were simple karaoke machines. We had what we called the author's corner. The children had to write a story or poem and then present their work to the class. The author sat in a rocking chair and read to the class. When they were finished, the class could ask the authors questions. Because we used the karaoke machine, the students listening could actually hear the author. Authoring became real, and the students were truly interested in each other's stories. It was like a famous person had come to class. Students were allowed to ask questions about the story. As time went by, the questions asked became very good. The students learned something about quality questions. The readers became more expressive with their oral reading and learned with shock that their work was receiving critical acclaim. Their writing and listening skills improved. The author's corner and karaoke were popular with everyone. It was a great tool. We purchased six machines for all classes to share. They were and still are in constant use.

Another technology we used a lot was the video camera. The first time we used a camera was in third grade. Several teachers agreed to summarize three stories from our reading text in one big production. Each of the stories took place long ago: One was about the *Titanic*, one about the volcano that buried Pompeii under a sea of lava, and the third was all about an explosion that almost destroyed Boston. We divided the 60 children into three groups to tell all three stories. Since all three stories required us to go back in time, we selected three roving reporters to serve as today's link with the other time periods. We discovered a camera technique to go back in time, and then allowed the students to work in groups to write scripts for themselves. The teachers trained the students in the necessary skills of, and assisted in, the editing process. The groups included video training, interview methods, computer skills, set designing, and prop and crew training. Altogether, there were six teachers collaborating on the project. We took a week to plan, write, practice, and make the video. All the students watched as each took their turn in front of the camera. It was "quiet on the set" and listen for cues. The students had access to the same body of knowledge and all had the real-life experience of being actors as well. The end product was wonderful, and all enjoyed watching it together with some popcorn on the side.

WebQuests are another way for a class to use technology. In my fourth-grade class, we used a Web site we found to help our children read the story of *Sarah, Plain and Tall* (MacLachlan, 1985). We live in a rural community, and many of our children have no concept of the two main settings of the story. We felt we had to build a background for them. I used Google to find the WebQuest that would be the most helpful. Students could independently go to the WebQuest and see photos and live camera shots of the Maine coastline as well as the grasslands and dunes of the prairie. They also had information on the animals and vegetation of these geographical areas. Students could really take the time to compare and contrast the lives and experiences of the main characters. The quest had activities and questions for the students about the content of the story. They enjoyed having laptops at their own desks and working as teams to answer the questions. I found that students' reading improved and that they were really motivated to do their assignments and review reading and writing skills.

For the past three years, we have added a new type of technology to our fourth-grade reading program. We call it the WGES-TV News. Each morning, two students from the fourth grade lead the Pledge of Allegiance and read the daily announcements to the school. As a reading teacher, I initiated this project to teach presentation skills to students. The fourth English language arts skill is speaking, and it is often left out of curricula in the early grade levels. Each week, two new students are sent to the studio to do the news. I see them before the broadcast to go over the script and give presentation tips. Usually, the first day, the students are very nervous and hearts are pounding. I make sure the script is color-coded and bolded or underlined for emphasis. They practice for 15 minutes to be sure they can pronounce all the words and gain confidence. As the week goes on, they begin to read longer articles and add little tidbits of their own. We call this editing and revising. In class, this task is dreadfully dull, but in the newsroom, students see how using these skills can improve the broadcast and help to get the message across to the listeners.

All too often, children read aloud in class without considering the purpose of reading aloud. They think that reading fast means they are good readers. They don't consider that they are really delivering the author's message. I find that some fourth graders cannot say the Pledge of Allegiance slowly with feeling and emphasis. They only know how to rattle it off at a fast pace. When they are forced to slow down, many of the younger children can't remember the words. We found we had to post a cue card in the studio to help them say the words correctly.

All students doing the news learn something about presentation skills, but not all learn the same thing. Some just gain confidence as readers. Some learn to read sentence-by-sentence and not word-by-word. Some learn to read with emphasis, and others learn to establish eye contact with their audience. Some students learn to dress properly and to be on time. Still others learn how to sit still and listen for cues. This is truly learning by doing and on-the-job training. We record each show and allow the presenting students to watch and critique the broadcast daily. Oftentimes, they see and correct some imperfections on their own. It's a great opportunity for all involved and a benefit to our school.

Over my 29-year career, I have found technology to be a great tool for teachers and students alike. In order to use technology, I needed to be a risk taker and be willing to make mistakes and keep trying. I also needed to learn the technology I was using and had to be willing to spend some time on my own practicing the new skills to become proficient and confident. The term *life-long learner* certainly applies to teachers when it comes to technology. When I first started teaching, schools had no computers. Our school had no video cameras and no idea that there could be an Internet. We've come a long way, and I have loved every inch of the journey. I would like to encourage others to try some of these ideas. Technology really does give "life" to all students as they learn, those who struggle and need the motivation and those who are bright and need the challenge. Technology is a wonderful tool for everyone!

Reference

MacLachlan, P. (1985). *Sarah, plain and tall.* New York: Harper & Row.

ℕ 12. Technological Inventions Research and PowerPoint Project

LeAnn Morris
Carson City, Nevada

Recommended Level: Grades 3–5

Overall Objective: To help students understand how inventions have affected history, using Internet research and PowerPoint presentations.

Living in the Knowledge Age, it is important for our students to understand how we have progressed to modern times and what inventions have lead us to how we live today. Using the Internet to research information about a technological invention of their choice allows the students many different resources in one convenient place. With time constraints always an issue in a computer lab, the Internet is the wisest choice for the research component of this project. The end product of the project is a Microsoft PowerPoint slideshow. This project integrates social studies, language arts, and technology standards and allows the students an opportunity to use real-world applications to research and share their knowledge.

I give my students nine 45-minute class periods to work on their invention projects. Four of the class periods are used to research the chosen invention on the Internet and to complete the guided note taker. My students use an attached list of Internet sites that I preplan for them, which allows them to complete the research in the given time frame. Three class periods are used to complete the Microsoft PowerPoint presentations, and two class periods are used to present the projects to the class. The students choose their own groups of three to work together. Each student has a different task each class period: typing notes on the guided note taker, searching Internet sites for information, and building the presentation. Each student knows what his or her role is through a rotation system that is established during the first class of the project, and each student knows what the expectations are for each class.

I have learned from past research projects that if I can help focus my students' attention and provide them with a guideline of what is important, this leads to much greater productivity during the lesson.

This is why I created the guided note taker template. My students learn much more in a shorter amount of class time with this research project. By having their attention centered on exactly what I need them to learn to meet the lesson objective, they also increase the quality and quantity of the work produced by each group of students.

I reinforce legal and ethical issues with the students throughout the project with lesson directions and reminders about the emphasis and importance of proper citation of Internet sites. I always tell my students, "Give credit where credit is due." We also discuss file security and how anyone who uses a school computer can have access to their work, because there is no password protection. I also remind all students about the AUP (Acceptable Use Policy) they signed and have on file for responsible computer and Internet use at school; and I tell them how important it is to always be conscientious of the actions and choices they make. I model to my students how to cite Internet resources using the Web site Citing Web Resources (http://library.lafayette.edu/help/citing/webpages). I also use the following Web sites to model importance of Internet safety and security: www.staysafeonline.org, www.ikeepsafe.org, www.staysafe.org, www.isafe.org, www.safekids.com and www.protectkids.com. I share this list of Internet sites with the parents.

Assessment of this unit is done using a variety of formats. Using the Internet site Rubistar (http://rubistar.4teachers.org/index.php) I create a Research Rubric and a PowerPoint Rubric for grading. Students are graded based on the criteria presented to them on the rubrics. I evaluate the Internet sites that my students use to get their information to make sure they are trusted and reliable sources by using Kathy Shrock's (2002) *The ABC's of Website Evaluation.* During the project, I have at least one whole-group discussion about what criteria makes a good Internet site, and then I work individually with each small group on a daily basis. I also give guidance on Internet sites that contain false information and how to confirm the accuracy and validity based on *The ABC's of Website Evaluation.*

Assessment is also done by eliciting high student engagement through constant monitoring and observation, whether it is informally walking around the room; enabling SmartTech Synchroneyes, our lab monitoring software; or from student and peer evaluations. Having the students work in groups of three also allows them to choose who they work with, allowing for adjustments to be made in group dynamics to promote sharing responsibilities equally for completing and presenting the finished slide shows.

Helpful Tips

Students should have prior knowledge and experience with Microsoft Word, Microsoft PowerPoint, and how to use the Internet. To adapt to younger students, choose the research topic for them and have a list of topic-specific Internet sites already bookmarked in the computers to allow easier access for the research.

Reference

Shrock, K. (2002). *The ABC's of website evaluation*. Discovery Education. Retrieved April 05, 2009, from http://school.discovery education.com/schrockguide/pdf/weval_02.pdf

13. Video Production in the Classroom

Michael Flynn
Southampton, Massachusetts

Recommended Level: Grades K–5+

Overall Objective: Tackle video productions with your students, and watch them become actively involved in learning, rather than passively watching films. Start with something simple, like a short play.

When I think back to when I was in elementary school, I remember watching many movies. This was back in the 1980s, when we still had the reel-to-reel projectors, so the only exciting part of watching a film was having the chance to flick the switch to start it.

When I became a teacher, I was impressed by the sheer size of the VHS library in our school and began utilizing videos in class. However,

I soon discovered that, like my experience in elementary school, the students became very passive during the videos and only became excited when I needed someone to push play.

Although videos can be an excellent complement to a great unit of study, students often have a low level of engagement in them. Therefore, I have become highly selective of the videos that my students view, and I show very few of them.

Instead, my students create their own videos throughout the year in the form of a bimonthly television show. Each time we finish a unit of study, I break the children into small groups and assign them a specific topic we have covered. They must work together to create a segment (skit, newscast, experiment, etc.) that will teach their topic to the audience. They write scripts, rehearse, and create backgrounds and props often on their own time at home or at recess. I then film them and edit the material at home on my computer. I add music, sound effects, titles, and transitions to the footage and then burn one DVD for each student in the class.

We air the television show through our internal cable network for the whole school to see, and my students become minor celebrities for the day. It is not uncommon for them to have to sign autographs on their bus ride home. We also have a special screening of the production for families, complete with popcorn and juice.

The students end up watching their production over and over again as they share it with family and friends. Each time, they solidify the knowledge that is imbedded in it. Additionally, they had to go above and beyond typical learning expectations in order to create the production in the first place. This has been an effective way to enhance the instruction in my classroom, and my students love it.

I must state that putting together a whole television show complete with various segments and other material is quite a leap from where I began doing video production in the classroom. If you are new to video production, start with something simple, and let your projects evolve as your skills develop.

To get started, I strongly suggest trying an easy production, like a short play, as they are intended for performances on a stage. This eliminates the issue of camera angles, because all of the action happens in one area. Therefore, you simply have to mount a camera on a tripod and leave it stationary for the whole production.

Preproduction

During your language arts block, begin by having the class draft ideas for a play. This does not have to be too elaborate. Simply stating main characters, settings, problems, and resolutions are enough to get things rolling. When there is agreement on a plan, you must then flesh the material out a bit. A character must be created for each student (including narrators), and details need to develop. Depending on the age of your students, this might be all the work you do for one session.

Once a detail plan is created, the process of writing can begin. I use the shared writing technique where the students say what to write, but I act as the scribe. This speeds the process along but keeps the ownership of the product with the students. Our first round of writing has a focus on narration only. The children simply tell the story without trying to fit in dialog. As they say sentences, I write each one on a sentence strip rather than on chart paper. This is essential if you want to seamlessly add dialog to the piece. I would also suggest using a specific color strip for all the narration.

With the story written, it is time to add the dialog. I try to keep things as equitable as possible, so I often have a set number of lines for each student. If I decide each student will have four lines, I give them each four-sentence strips. I also try to make each student's strip unique either in the color of the strip or the color of the crayon they use to write. That way, when the piece is put together, everyone can identify his or her section. They then have to write their character's name followed by a colon on each one.

Next, we start reading the story one sentence at a time. After each sentence, we talk about what is happening and if characters should be talking. If there are stage directions suggested, I write them down on chart paper. If dialog is to occur, the students write their lines on their sentence strips.

Of course, some students will need more lines than other, depending on their character, but it helps to have a set limit. Then students have to be very careful in the lines they choose for themselves. I believe it makes the writing better. On these same lines, I must also point out that as the teacher, you are in charge of quality control. Do not hesitate to make suggestions or changes if the writing is not clear or relevant. I am a big proponent of student ownership, but we are also teachers and want them to learn effective writing strategies.

Once this process is finished, you should have your whole play on sentence strips. I use my endless supply of magnetic clips to post all of the strips on the chalkboard. Depending on time and the length of the play, you may want students to have individual scripts to take home and practice. I have a parent volunteer come in to type the script once we've posted it on the board.

With the play written, it's time to focus on the settings, costumes, and props. I work closely with our art teacher on these projects, and she designs and creates backgrounds and props with my students during their art time. I leave costuming up to the students and their families. Most have old Halloween costumes and so on that they donate for our productions. While this work is being developed, the students are also constantly rehearsing their lines at home or during one of their literature centers in class.

At this stage, it is time to begin considering the technical aspect of the project. You should find a spot in the classroom for your set and then have the students hang the backdrop and set up props. Position the camera where you intend to shoot the production, and be sure everything is in view. However, if you are using the microphone that is built into the camera, remember that the farther you are away from students, the harder it will be to hear them. This is an intricate balancing act between seeing the whole set and hearing all of the students.

Have the students rehearse in front of the camera to get used to it and for you to practice your directing skills. I find it helpful to put tape on the floor on both sides of the set just outside of the camera's view. That way, students know whether or not they are on camera. As students rehearse, remind them to project their voice, face the front, and look natural. These simple reminders make a big difference in the production.

Production

When it is time to film, place a sign outside your classroom door indicating that filming is happening. That way you won't have interruptions ruin a good take. Make sure you have a full tape in the camera and that the camera is plugged in or has a full battery charge. Most important, have some independent work for your students to do quietly while they are not on camera. This will limit behavior issues and disruptions. It also allows for all students to be productive at one time.

When you push the record button on the camera, wait five seconds before giving the signal to begin. Also, when the scene is finished, allow five seconds before you push the button to stop recording. This will make a world of difference when you are editing. Begin recording the scenes, and keep track of each time you record (scene one, take one, etc.). Mark on your notes which take was the good one, and then move on. Don't worry about the mistakes, because they make great material to show as outtakes at the end of your video.

Postproduction

When the play has been taped, the hard work is about to begin. If you have older students, many are probably naturals at editing on the computer. However, if you are like me, you end up doing it yourself. This work can be technical, and I cannot explain it all right here, so I will give the basics and allow you to pursue the technical issues on your own.

You have to stream the video into your computer using a Firewire cable and the video editing software of your choice. If you are a new to this, you can use the free, basic software that comes with your operating system (Windows Movie Maker or iMovie). The basic software is designed for use by amateurs and is very intuitive. If you would like something a little more professional, I would suggest Adobe Premiere Elements for PC and Final Cut Express for Mac.

With the video streamed in, you can now begin to edit. First, you must cut out all of the outtakes so you have a rough cut of your good takes. If you have funny outtakes, stick them at the end of the video instead of deleting them. Now, it is time to add transitions between clips. Transitions are like spices in that too much variety ruins the dish. Keep it simple and consistent so as not to distract the audience.

When your play is edited with transitions, it is time to add a sound track and sound effects. This is not essential, but it makes a world of difference. It is important to note that you need to use open source material in order for your production to avoid breaking copyright laws. Do a Web search for open source music or sounds, and a whole bunch of sites will pop up. Some cost money, while others are free. As always, be careful what you download. I prefer to purchase CDs with open source soundtracks and sound effects.

Once the editing is done, you must then burn it to a DVD. The higher-end software already has that capability built in, but the low-end ones require another program. Macs have iDVD as part of the package, so you do not have to purchase anything extra, but Windows does not. If you are editing in Movie Maker, you need to buy DVD burning software.

With the production complete, you can now show it to the class, the school, students' families, and others. Everyone will be impressed by it, and the students will love it. Each time you do a production, it gets easier. Over time, you may get to a level where you want to create a television show that teaches the content your students have learned. This is a highly effective way to engage kids in authentic learning, and the memories will be theirs forever.

Helpful Tips

- Practice editing a simple slideshow with pictures before you take on a video production. Slideshows are much easier to edit and have fewer variables. This will give you some time to become comfortable with the editing tools and the software.
- Expect the unexpected. Video production has many unforeseen quirks and issues that arise, and you must be ready to deal with them. They might be small issues like not finishing the taping in one day and having to finish the next day, when kids are in different outfits. They could be big issues, like an error somewhere in the production is preventing it from burning to DVD.
- Keep it simple, and keep it short. You do not want to spend a week at home editing your production. Although the end result would be great, we all have lives and will not be up for Oscar nominations with our work.

- Try to shoot the video in the order that you will edit it. This will save time during the postproduction process, as you won't have to sequence all of the scenes.
- As you improve your skills in video production, consider upgrading equipment and software to broaden your capabilities. Microphones, lighting, green screens, and a nice camera make a world of difference. They also provide many teaching opportunities, as students learn how they work and begin to use them effectively.

PART II

Teaching Science and Math

Teaching Science

Overview, Chapters 14–22

14. **Karin Huttsell,** a first-grade teacher from Ft. Wayne, Indiana, uses the story of the three little pigs to teach how easily certain objects are moved by air currents. This science lesson makes a great follow-up to a unit on fairy tales.

15. **Marianne Sipe**, a second-grade teacher from Goodlettsville, Tennessee, builds a birdfeeder with her class and observes the wildlife it brings outside their classroom window. Students learn about the food chain, local birds, squirrels, and other creatures, and they keep wildlife notebooks to improve their observation skills.

16. **Carol Brueggeman**, a science and math resource teacher from Colorado Springs, Colorado, asks students to become the experts during her African animal unit. The students teach the class and take charge of their learning. When the unit culminates in a trip to the zoo, people outside of the class will stop and listen to the students present their information.

17. **Diana A. Minor,** a special services teacher in Hannibal, Missouri, explores tap and bottled water with a blind taste test conducted by her science class. Students get hands-on experience at conducting an experiment and learn about protecting the environment by drinking tap water.

18. **Wendy Smith,** a kindergarten through fifth-grade math, science, and technology specialist from Webster, New York, works with students to monitor the local water quality. Students act as environmental scientists taking water samples and studying the macroinvertebrates and other creatures that live in the pond.

19. **Freida Taylor Aiken** is an elementary school gifted teacher in Aiken, Georgia, who writes mysteries for her students to solve using clues she prepares. Find out who stole the famous Hope Pearl—was it Sandy Shipley, found with brand A duct tape, or Shelly Boatwright, found with traces of sand and brand B duct tape? Watch as your students turn into forensic scientists hot on the trail of a wanted diamond thief, and learn investigative skills along the way.

20. **Nancy Bryant** is an elementary school teacher in Supply, North Carolina, who incorporates local environmental issues into her science curriculum through a study of the loggerhead turtles on the North Carolina coast. Nancy combines community service, literature, math, and technology in a month-long unit that culminates in a trip to Top Sail Beach to help researchers release 20 sea turtles back into the wild.

21. **Amy Nicholl**, a fifth-grade teacher in Windsor, Colorado, uses the inquiry method to engage students in science. Amy's lesson on the laws of motion integrate the other subject areas into the science curriculum through student-created journals modeled after Lewis and Clark's, fictional stories submitted by students about Isaac Newton, and nonfiction reading on Newton's laws.

22. **Debbie Easley**, a teacher in Somerville, Alabama, guides her fifth-grade students through a series of stations using inquiry to answer questions. At each station, they work through the steps of a scientific investigation and record questions and data in their science journal.

14. Huff and Puff

Karin Huttsell
Ft. Wayne, Indiana

Recommended Level: Grades K–2

Overall Objective: To foster scientific inquiry in the early grades. Students will demonstrate that some objects can be moved easily by air, and some cannot, using their breath to create movement with different objects.

Standards Met (Indiana):

Science: Understanding about scientific inquiry, properties of objects and materials, position, and motion of objects

Materials Needed:

- Copy of the story *The 3 Little Pigs*
- Straw
- Sticks
- Brick
- Ping-pong balls
- Masking tape
- Recording sheets

This science activity makes a great follow-up to a study of fairy tales. Read the story of *The 3 Little Pigs* to the students. Lead the students in a discussion about the wolf and why he was able to blow some of the houses down but not the brick house. You can also encourage the students to discuss the different building materials in the story and attributes of each material. This would be a good time to set the straw, sticks, and brick on a table for students to explore. Explain that some things can be moved easily by air currents. Have students generate a list of things that can be moved easily by air. Go over the rules for scientific inquiry—make an observation that the straw is lighter than the brick, make a prediction as "I think I can blow the straw," conduct an experiment testing which things can be moved by blowing on them, draw a conclusion as to why the brick could not be moved by blowing on it, and communicate the results as recording and/or telling a partner what you found out. Let students make predictions about the straw, sticks, and brick.

Next, pair students and let them experiment with some straw, some sticks, and a brick. Place the objects on the table. Let each partner take turns moving the objects by blowing on them (like the Big Bad Wolf). Provide time for students to draw conclusions about which items were easily moved and which were not. Use the recording sheet to document the results. Students can do further experiments to see how objects move and how air currents can be controlled. Use the masking tape and tape simple shapes on the floor, such as a square, a circle, and a triangle. The shapes should be about three feet wide and long. Give students a ping-pong ball. Allow students to experiment moving the ball around the shapes taped on the floor using their breath. Let students try different shapes, and encourage them to test ways to keep the ball inside the masking tape. Give students some questions to ponder, such as, "Why did the ball wander off of the shape? What happens when you blow too hard? What helped you control the ball and keep it on the shape? Why did your partner use more breaths to get the ball around the shape than you did? Would a bigger ball be easier or harder to blow? Is one shape harder to blow a ball around than another shape?" Students can record how many breaths it took to get the ball around each shape. Let students share their conclusions and thoughts about their experiments.

HelpfulTips

You may need to watch students with asthma during this experiment so that they do not have any adverse reactions. You can adapt this for younger students by allowing them to test only two things, such as straw and a brick. Younger students can easily blow a single piece of straw. Both older and younger students will discover that the brick can't be moved by their breath. Older students should be able to determine that shorter breaths help with the control of the ping-pong ball. Older students will be able to expand the experiment by using different objects to concentrate their airflow, like blowing through a drinking straw. Older students are capable of writing down the steps of the experiment and the conclusions. Older students can also experiment with a partner to see which one can blow a piece of straw or a stick off of a table first. This could lead to a high-quality discussion about wind forces such as tornadoes and hurricanes.

---

15. Awareness of Wildlife

Marianne Sipe
Goodlettsville, Tennessee

Recommended Level: Grades 1–3

Overall Objective: Encourages students to use math, reading, and writing in scientific discovery of backyard wildlife.

Materials Needed:

- Birdfeed and suet
- Measuring cups
- Composition notebooks
- Books or other materials about birds

- Also nice but not strictly necessary, a digital camera and printer

Old Center Elementary is located in the suburbs of Metropolitan Nashville Public Schools. Our second-grade classroom is situated at the bottom of a grassy knoll. From our windows, we see lush green grass, beautiful trees, and a sidewalk with steps that lead up to the main building. It is the perfect place to observe wildlife up close from our windows. What teacher would not want to take advantage of the perfect setting for a scientific observatory for birds, squirrels, chipmunks, and a few hungry predators? This ideal setting was an inspiration for me to write a grant asking for funds to begin "Audubon Advocates."

The objective of my grant was to have students use math (measuring and graphing), reading (research), and writing (journaling) for scientific discovery of backyard wildlife. My grant request included eight birdfeeders, 20 pounds of birdfeed and suet, storage canisters for the seed, measuring cups, a digital camera, and a classroom printer for the photographs that we took of the birds. I also purchased several beautiful coffee table "backyard bird" books for classroom research.

My goal was for the students to be involved as much as possible with attracting wildlife. First, we placed and hung the feeders just 10 feet away from the windows. We took note of each feeder's capacity. The students drew diagrams in their notebooks of the tube feeders and the hopper feeders. With our measuring cups, we accurately measured the amounts of birdseed it would take to fill each feeder. After identifying the many different seeds, each student took part in the measuring process for each feeder. (They enjoyed sinking their hands down in the big canisters full of various seeds!) We took pictures of ourselves in the preparatory process and glued them in our notebooks. We then wrote captions for each picture. The students loved receiving pictures of themselves and then being able to write about performing an actual scientific task.

It took several days for the birds to start coming to our classroom window. Once they came, the students' excitement was immeasurable! The cardinals came first, then the chickadees, and the titmouse. Squirrels and chipmunks soon fought over the feeders. Alas, the black cat came and we saw first hand how cruel nature can be. It was the food chain at work right before our eyes! We took pictures of all that we saw and again glued them into our bird notebooks. We added captions to each picture using rich vocabulary such as *prey, predator,* and *consumer.* Again, the photographs of themselves and the birds were great motivational tools for the students to write well-constructed sentences.

As the project progressed and school ended, maintaining our notebooks came from the data we collected from our observations and the research we did by reading about each bird. The students looked forward to each bird activity. They kept their bird journals, which were full of pictures of themselves that reminded them of the many activities they participated in for "Audubon Advocates."

16. Student-Expert Groups

Carol Brueggeman
Colorado Springs, Colorado

Recommended Level: Grade 2

Overall Objective: To allow students to guide their own learning of different zoo animals, and to have them demonstrate expertise by teaching other students about an animal.

Standards Met (Colorado):

Science: Life science; Earth science

Materials Needed:

- A variety of reference materials on the designated topics
- Note cards or paper for final notes
- Markers, crayons, and/or colored pencils for space activity
- Materials groups need for zoo activity

Zoo Expert—Groups

Student-expert groups allow students to take charge of their own learning. Students are responsible for teaching the other students in the class. The expert group idea can be used with any topic that allows research to be part of the focus. I will describe using the expert groups as part of a field experience at the zoo. During the zoo visit, the students not only present factual information but also design an activity that demonstrates one of the facts about the animal. I have used the expert-group idea with students second grade and above.

The teacher decides which animals will be visited at the zoo. It is not necessary to see the whole zoo during a visit. For example, you could concentrate on African animals or animals in a specific food web, or any other group or combination that coincides with your curriculum. Our fifth grade concentrates on the African animals housed in our zoo. The zoo has a large number of these animals, such as lions, elephants, hippos, giraffe, kudus, warthogs, meerkats, and a few others. Students will present the information about the animal and do the activity in front of the animal displays at the zoo.

Students are divided into groups of three or four. Each group becomes experts on one specific animal. The students research a variety of materials to find facts about their assigned animal. They also try to find or design an activity that demonstrates something unique about the animal. I remind them to keep the activity simple because they must take the materials with them on the trip to the zoo.

The expert-group members must each have a set of fact cards and materials for the activity. During the actual zoo trip the "experts" are in separate groups. Each zoo group will have one of the experts on each animal in it. The zoo group visits all the animals for which there is an expert. Each zoo group starts at a different display so the groups are presenting at separate places. At each animal display, the expert presents the facts about the animal and has the other students do the activity. Many times during the zoo trip, people not with our group stop to listen to the students present information and want to try the activity.

The most important part of organizing the trip is to make sure you have at least one adult for each zoo group and enough materials for the activities, as students will be in many sections of the zoo.

This an organization chart for the zoo trip and some activities that have been used by my students. There is one expert on each animal in each group.

Zoo Groups starting at different displays

1	2	3	4
Lion	Elephant	Giraffe	Gorilla
Elephant	Hippo	Old World Monkeys	Giraffe
Giraffe	Lion	Gorilla	Hippo
Gorilla	Old World Monkeys	Elephant	Lion
Hippo	Giraffe	Orangutan	Old World Monkeys
Old World Monkeys	Orangutan	Lion	Orangutan
Orangutan	Gorilla	Hippo	Elephant

This schedule allows the students to visit animal displays at different times and makes each expert responsible for teaching the other students in the zoo group about the animal he/she has researched.

Sample activities presented by the students:

- Giraffe—Demonstrate the height of a giraffe by using a string 15 to 16 feet long. Use masking tape to flag one student's height on the string. From that flag, mark another student's height. Do this until the string ends. This represents how many students would have to stand on top of each other's heads to stand as tall as a giraffe.
- Hippos—Ask students to close their nostrils, move their ears, and hold their breath at the same time. Hippos do this when they are in the water. You can also have the other students try to eat string licorice without using their teeth. This is how hippos eat grass.

- Gorillas—Compare a gorilla's body structure to a human's. Use a five and one-half foot piece of ribbon to represent the gorilla's body height. Have one student stand on one end and another student pull it to its full height. Use another piece of ribbon six and one-half feet long to represent the gorilla's arm span. Ask two students to pull the ribbon to its full width across the chest of the student standing on the first ribbon. This gives a visual of the gorilla's height compared to its arm span.
- Old World Monkeys—Use a variety of pictures, die-cuts, or real objects. Have the other students separate the food into two piles—what the monkeys will eat and what they will not eat. The expert then shows the correct foods the old world monkeys eat.

After the zoo trip (usually the next day), each zoo group creates a poster report on the facts they learned about each animal they visited. This allows the teacher to make sure each expert presented the same information.

The expert-group strategy works with curricular areas in which the students can research topics and share the information. It is a nice change for students to be responsible for teaching each other. I also find that they listen carefully to each other and show each other respect during the reporting.

17. What's It Worth to You?

Diana A. Minor
Hannibal, Missouri

Recommended Level: Grades 2–3

Overall Objective: This water testing activity teaches not only the inquiry method for science but also engages students in consumer math as well. The students will perform four tests on various bottled and tap waters to determine which water is the best purchase.

Standards Met (Missouri):

Math: Represent data using pictures and bar graphs

Science: Use of science process skills, scientific knowledge, scientific investigation, reasoning, and critical thinking; Able to formulate a testable question and explanation and to select appropriate investigative methods in order to obtain evidence relevant to the explanation; Plan and conduct a simple investigation to answer a question

Materials Needed:

- 10 index cards—write the name of each water on cards 1–5; write the cost per gallon on cards 6–10
- 4 brands of commercially bottled water (Aquafina, Great Value, Dasani, etc.) and 1 bottle of tap water
- per group; remove the labels and number the bottles 1–5
- 5 five-ounce cups per student numbered 1–5
- One table test sheet and one sheet of graph paper per student

Because bottled water is becoming so popular, it is important that students recognize the reasons why bottled water is purchased and realize the cost of bottled water versus tap water. Through the testing procedures, the students will be able to determine the best buy for their money and evaluate the pros and cons of being consumers of bottled water.

Divide the students into groups. At each group, place the five bottles of water on the table. Inform the class that tests have consistently found that tap water is as healthy for you as bottled water. Bottled water can cost as much as 500 times the price of tap water! Explain that today we are going to do a taste and cost test on bottled water. Ask the students:

How many of you or your parents drink bottled water?

What brand of water do you drink?

Why do you drink that particular brand of water?

List the questions on the board for all of the class to see, and then write several of the answers under the appropriate question.

Tell the students that we are going to rate the different kinds of water with five variables, using a scoring scale of 1–5, with 1 being the lowest/poorest and 5 being the highest/best. The variables will be Smell, Taste, Aftertaste, Package, Appeal, and Cost. We will then add up the total score for each water sample to determine which water is the best purchase. The highest possible score is 25. Remember, you may only use each number once. For instance, if you give the first sample a 1 in taste, the second sample can only have a 2, 3, 4, or 5 in taste. Use a different testing cup to taste each water source. Supply the students with the cost to fill in on the testing tables.

	Smell	Taste	Aftertaste	Package	Appeal	Cost	Total
Water 1							
Water 2							
Water 3							
Water 4							
Water 5							

After the students have tested each water sample and tallied their scores, have the class give the results by asking, "How many students chose number one as their favorite?" and so on. Put the totals on the board to determine which water was chosen by the most classmates. Provide the students the names of the various waters, including the tap water! Discuss the following questions:

1. Which water was the most popular?

2. Which water was the least popular?

3. Which result was the most surprising?

4. What are the pros of using bottled water?

5. What are the cons of using bottled water?

Under cons, be sure to list the environmental impacts such as pollution (littering with the old bottles), overfilling of already crowded landfills, the creation of more plastic, and so on. There is also the health impact . . . bottled water does not contain fluoride, and hence more cavities for children drinking only bottled water. The cost factor! For what you pay for a bottle of water, you could purchase enough tap water to fill a 666-gallon tank! Also, if you are spending $4.00 a day for bottled water . . . that is $1,400 a year!

In the past six years that I have been conducting this experiment with my students, they have consistently chosen the school's drinking fountain water (tap water) as their favorite! It is always a huge surprise to them, and this really is an effective tool to help them realize . . . "What's it worth to you?"

18. Pond Partners

Water Quality Investigations

Wendy Smith
Webster, New York

Recommended Level: Grades 2–4

Overall Objective: In this yearlong project coordinated by a team of teachers, students develop and implement their own scientific inquiry investigations tied to water sampling activities and seasonal changes in the park. Students learn how to develop hypotheses, collect and document data using current technology and equipment, and analyze and present the data to others.

Standards Met (New York):

Analysis, inquiry, and design: Use scientific inquiry to post questions, seek answers, and develop solutions

Information systems: Will access, generate, process, and transfer information using appropriate technologies

Inquiry and process skills: Classifying, communicating, gathering, and organizing data, observing, predicting

Interconnectedness: Common themes

Interdisciplinary problem solving

Materials Needed:

- Data Collection Tools: Vernier Lab Quest with temperature, pH, and dissolved oxygen sensors or Pasco PASPORT AirLink Sensor Interface to use with Palm Tungsten E2 handheld and temperature, pH, and dissolved oxygen sensors
- Digital cameras
- iPods with voice recorders
- GPS to mark data locations
- Specimen pans
- Hand lenses
- Digital microscope
- Stream nets
- Turbidity tube
- Flow rate test equipment (measured string, ping-pong ball, stopwatch)

Introduction

The poet William B. Yeats once said, "Education is not filling a bucket, but lighting a fire." The team of five teachers working on this project made our community parks the onsite locations for a yearlong data collection program designed to ignite learning for second through fourth graders' living environment science curriculum. The "Pond Partners" project helped the students connect hands-on experiences with conceptual understanding. Acting as environmental scientists, they discovered the hidden world of macroinvertebrates in our local ponds and stream and from this investigation developed an understanding of the importance of clean, fresh water on our entire ecosystem. Onsite field observations and water quality sampling occurred throughout the year, and classrooms developed their own inquiry-based investigations to further deepen their content understandings and enhance their scientific process skills. Students explored life cycles of macroinvertebrates, invasive species of Lake Ontario, and issues regarding potable water.

Classroom Preparations

Before setting out to conduct field studies in the parks, we provided opportunities for students to become familiar with the probeware and handheld computers by conducting investigations in the classroom. To start off, we explored how to use temperature sensors in conjunction with their handhelds through an investigation that revolved around the question, "Does shade affect the water temperature?"

We shared stories about sitting under the shade of a large tree during a very hot day. Pictures were shown on the interactive whiteboard, as visual aids during the discussion, to guide students' hypotheses.

For our practice investigation, we reviewed the materials we needed and the procedures that we would be using. Then we prepared two containers of water and set one in a sunny spot while the other container was placed under the shade of a large tree. We used the handhelds and temperature sensors to record the initial temperature of the water and took additional temperature readings at two 10-minute intervals.

While waiting to collect the data at the 10- and 20-minute marks, the class learned that shade from the vegetation surrounding streams, called *riparian vegetation,* is an important part of keeping bodies of water cool. Areas with adequate shade keep cooler than those exposed to sunlight, and they support different types of wildlife. Overhanging grasses, shrubs and trees, even debris in the water, provide shade that keeps the water cool.

The children were prompted to conduct group discussions about other conditions surrounding a body of water that would affect its temperature. Their ideas were then shared with the class. Possible conditions included

- Depth of the water
- Width of the body of water
- Seasonal conditions
- Speed of the water
- Time of day
- Amount of sunlight

While we reviewed the steps for the completed experiment, students were asked if they had any new questions about temperature that they would like to investigate. It was also explained that the experiments should be set up to allow for the changing of only one variable.

Finally, we evaluated the investigation via three journal prompts: "What tools do scientists use to measure temperature?" "What are the common units that temperature is measured in?" and, "When would it be necessary or important to measure or report water temperature data?"

Similar procedures were used to introduce the children to the pH and dissolved oxygen sensors. These experiences provided students with the technology skills necessary to conduct their fieldwork, and also spurred students to ask new questions to answer using the tools.

To help students practice identifying macroinvertebrates and use a dichotomous key, stream samples were brought to the classroom, and using a document camera, the organisms were projected onto an interactive whiteboard. Seeing the organisms on the board made it much simpler for the initial practice with identification, using the key and counting the number of each. Students also discovered how different organisms are found in different types of water quality and began to wonder how healthy the water would be at their data collection locations throughout the year.

Since we wanted students to be able to easily record observations in the field, we taught the students how to use an iPod with a voice recorder to document data-collection activities and to make observations about seasonal changes, human impact—positive and negative— and to ask questions while working at the ponds and streams. Practice with the digital cameras was also part of our classroom lessons prior to heading outside.

Data Collection, Observations, and Analysis

Once they were proficient at collecting data, students ventured into the field to test and evaluate the water quality at local parks. They worked in groups at various locations to collect air, water, and soil temperature data, as well as measure pH and dissolved oxygen levels. A turbidity tube was used to measure water quality, and a flow rate test was also conducted at several points along the stream. Students documented the streambed composition and the vegetation along the side of the stream using the digital cameras and iPods with voice recorders.

Macroinvertebrates samples were collected and distributed to small groups of students to identify, count, and record their findings. Once this task was completed, samples were returned to the stream.

In addition to the data collection, the children documented their observations of positive or negative human impact (for example, garbage in the water), examples of seasonal change (leaves lying on the ground), and examples of the connections between living organisms (fish) and their nonliving environment (water). Some students also created drawings of their observations or made field journals. Back in the classroom, we logged the data into a table, and they all analyzed the data to identify patterns and trends.

On-site visits were conducted in the fall, winter, and spring. Students were able to compare and contrast the data from previously collected data. The excursions helped solidify the children's understanding of seasonal changes in our local environment. The tasks of recording, reporting, and graphing of findings were tie-ins to the science concepts of change, cycles, and interdependence.

By observing the world around them, these elementary students were able to draw conclusions, make crosscurricular connections, and think broadly about the concepts they explored. In addition, they developed their critical thinking by asking new questions and answering those questions through research and testing.

During our first on-site visit, second graders were amazed at the number of macroinvertebrates discovered. Students wondered what their parents knew about invertebrates and they designed a survey to take home, collected data, and graphed and analyzed results. They classified the invertebrates according to their life cycle (complete or incomplete metamorphosis) and designed their own "new" macroinvertebrate life cycle. Students are still wondering, "Will we find different macroinvertebrates at different locations in the stream?"

While working with macroinvertebrates, third graders discovered a zebra mussel. Since it didn't look like the rest of the organisms, they were curious about what it was. With a little research, they found out that this small organism causes great problems. They had so many questions! We took the opportunity to explore their interest in depth. We found a Zebra Mussel Traveling Trunk (available from http://www.seagrant.umn.edu/educators/tt) to use, held a videoconference with a biologist, and conducted research using the Internet. They also created a survey for parents to find out how many of them were concerned about this invasive species. This has spurred them to ask new questions about other invasive species found in the Great Lakes.

We also had a guest speaker give a presentation on watersheds and potable water. Fourth graders had never heard the term and were curious about freshwater sources worldwide. Through their research, students became advocates of freshwater conservation and responsible use. One ingenious team even designed the PPD 5000 to purify water for countries with little or no potable water. They also created a survey to discover what adults knew about potable water and analyzed and graphed results. They were surprised at the lack of understanding by so many grown-ups.

Project Visibility

In addition to encouraging our ongoing scientific inquiries, we asked what a bona fide scientist does with the results of an experiment, and students realized that the information should be shared so that others could replicate the investigation.

- Students created a multimedia presentation to share with the Monroe County Water Coalition meeting held at the Brighton Town Hall. Representatives from each class attended the meeting and we used videoconferencing technology to connect the rest of the students back at our school to the meeting.
- Students presented at a school assembly. This session was streamed live over the Internet using Ustream.tv. We had viewers from across the country watching our live presentation and participating in the question/answer segment.
- Students also shared the presentation with our Webster Board of Education. These sessions are replayed on a local cable channel throughout the month.
- Students have handed out brochures they created with the HP grant project information and the wiki address (http://pondpartners .wikispaces.com).

- Students presented at the New York State Computers and Technology in Education (NYSCATE) annual conference in November 2008 in a student panel session.

Using Technology to Support Learning

One of our main objectives was to infuse technology into project lesson plans to engage learners, promote higher-order thinking skills, and provide authentic experiences. Using probeware and other technological observation and measuring devices, life and learning changed in the classroom. Students became immersed in science and worked like actual scientists, using real tools in authentic settings. Their investigations and studies had a purpose. Plus, it enabled the teachers to guide students toward a more curious or questioning approach to science by "making the commonplace intriguing" (Oliver, 2006, p. 25).

Since we were working with multiple classes and grade levels, we created a wiki for students and teachers to be able to work collaboratively. Students were able to write, revise, and discuss their learning using a shared online space and often worked on the project from home. Evidence of self-directed learning was apparent through the student discussions and posts added to the wiki (http://pondpartners .wikispaces.com).

One of the positive outcomes of the project was the teachers learning how to use various Web 2.0 tools to facilitate our project implementation and expand our professional learning network. We learned how to use Del.icio.us, a social bookmarking site, to share Internet sites related to the project. Google Docs was used for field trip planning, lesson plans, and reflections. The class wiki was incredibly valuable throughout the entire project, and members are thinking about ways to use this tool next year for various projects. Some of us have Google Reader accounts set up and subscribe to several educational blogs. Our enthusiasm for these tools and the way they have helped transform our practice has impacted others in our building who are also now interested in learning more about our project and what our students have accomplished.

Positive Results and Recognition

The Pond Partners project enabled students to use scientific inquiry from the very first day of school. By visiting the sites in the early fall, winter, and spring, they were able to continuously revisit their understandings of the natural phenomena that take place in our world.

Additionally, they learned how to identify variables and understand the difference between making observations versus inferences. Their natural curiosity led to the scientific inquiry that is imperative for self-directed learning. By making the learning experiences hands-on and authentic for the students, their desire to learn was set, the investigations and research held meaning for them, and they were excited about the "real" data that they were able to collect.

Student Quotes

I enjoyed the Pond Partners and how we used the handhelds. I like handhelds because I learned that it takes temperature. I like Pond Partners because they stick in groups. Also I liked that we got to go on field trips instead of looking at pictures and reading books. I like Pond Partners because we learned about the water temperature and macroinvertebrates.

Second-Grade Student

The Pond Partners Project was so much fun! I think it is really cool that we got to learn how to use an iPod, a digital camera, temperature probes and pH sensors. I have always wanted to use technology from the 21st century, and Pond Partners has let me do that! I learned about potable water, and now I will try to use it more wisely. Being able to see macroinvertebrates under the microscope really helped me learn about them. Just the sight of such cool technology makes a kid interested. It would be marvelous if more grades and classes got to do this. I know that fifth graders want to do this! Pond Partners opens doors to kids and the new technology around them!

Fourth-Grade Student

Reference

Oliver, A. (2006). *Creative teaching science in the early years and primary classroom.* London: David Fulton.

19. Using Mysteries to Teach Science Inquiry

Frieda Taylor Aiken
Jackson, Georgia

Recommended Level: Grades 2–4

Overall Objective: Students delve into the world of forensic science through teacher-created mysteries that teach content from several disciplines. The overall objective of this mystery unit is to focus on student understanding and use of scientific knowledge, ideas, and the inquiry process.

Standards Met (Georgia):

English Language Arts: Read a variety of print and nonprint texts to build an understanding of texts, of themselves, and of the cultures of the United States and of the world to acquire new information; To respond to the needs and demands of society and the workplace; Conduct research on issues and interests generating ideas and questions, and pose problems; Gather, evaluate, and synthesize data from a variety of sources to communicate discoveries in ways that suit the purpose and audience; Use a variety of technological and informational resources to gather and synthesize information and to create and communicate knowledge

Science: Able to do scientific inquiry; Understand properties of objects and materials; Understand the characteristics of organisms; Understand properties of earth materials; Understand about science and technology; Able to distinguish between natural objects and objects made by humans; Understand science as a human endeavor

Social Studies: Understand the world in spatial terms; Understand the physical processes that shape the patterns of Earth's surface

Materials Needed:

- Magnifying glasses of different sizes
- Dissecting microscopes with lights or hand-held lighted plastic scopes
- Plastic slides
- White school glue
- Several brands of duct tape
- Suspect sheet
- Alibi sheet
- World map
- Sand samples
- Fabricated letters from the director of the National Museum of Natural History

I like nothing better than curling up on my sofa with a mystery written by one of my favorite authors, and I enjoy trying to solve the mystery with each new twist and turn as the plot unfolds. I discovered this year that my students enjoy solving mysteries just as much as I do, and I have tackled the challenge of writing mysteries involving crimes for them to solve, using scientific inquiry, reasoning skills, and technology. I have had as much fun writing these mysteries as they have had solving them. The following is a mystery that my students solved involving the disappearance of the famous Hope Pearl. I include fabricated letters in the mystery from fictitious contact people, and my students receive a certificate of appreciation from that person after the mystery is solved.

The Case

The famous Hope Pearl has been stolen from the National Museum of Natural History in Washington, D.C. The crime occurred around 11:00 PM on the evening of February 13, 2008. The security guard was found bound and gagged with duct tape the following morning at 7:00 AM, when the daytime security guard arrived. The nighttime security guard had been hit on the head shortly after he arrived to work, and he lost consciousness. He could not identify the thief, but he knew that the crime had taken place around 11:00 PM because he had arrived a few minutes before 11:00 PM.

There will be four suspects, each with an alibi. There will also be clues left at the crime scene. It will be the students' job to accept the assignment as forensic scientists and work together in teams to solve the crime.

Sometime during the first day of the mystery, a letter will arrive addressed to the class from the director of the National Museum of Natural History. It will describe the nature of the crime and request the assistance of the students to solve the crime. They are instructed to write a letter to the director if they accept the assignment. All of the students will write a letter to the director accepting the assignment as a class, and the class will pick which student's letter will be "mailed" to the director. The remainder of day one will be spent preassessing the students' knowledge of how mysteries are solved and their knowledge of the use of microscopes and magnifying glasses. Students will be placed into groups of four to work together to research sand and duct tape. A class discussion will follow focusing on what the students have learned about sand and about duct tape that will help them solve this mystery.

Day two will be a time for the students to use the Internet to research the difference between organic and inorganic sand. The students will present group research reports on these topics to the class. Arrangements can also be made on day two for a forensic scientist to visit the class and discuss forensic procedures.

On day three, a letter will arrive from the director with photos of the crime scene and a description of each of the four suspects. The students will create a chart to keep on each suspect. The chart will include name of suspect, address of suspect, alibi, last time they were in Washington, D.C., hair color and type, brand of duct tape found in their home, and their knowledge of the Hope Pearl. The students will use the information the director sent to fill in the suspect charts.

Suspect Information Sheet

1. Sandy Shipley was born in Jacksonville, Florida, where she has lived her whole life. She has long straight blond hair. She dropped out of high school after tenth grade to dive for pearls. She has always dreamed of finding a perfect pearl. She attends all of the rare gem and pearl shows in the southeast part of the country, and she is the president of the local

chapter. She has visited the National Museum of Natural History 100 times to see the Hope Pearl. The last time she visited the museum was February 13, 2008. Duct tape brand A was found in her home.

2. Shelly Boatwright was born in Myrtle Beach, South Carolina, where she has lived her whole life. She has straight brown hair. She graduated from high school and attended the University of Charleston, where she majored in Biology. Shelly was kicked out of college because she spent so much time at the nearby beaches. She was obsessed with finding the largest pearl. She loves to visit the National Museum of Natural History to see the Hope Pearl, and she was last there on February 13, 2008. Duct tape brand B was found in her home.

3. Pearl Driftwood was born on San Salvador Island in the Bahamas, where she lived until she graduated from high school. She moved to Washington, D.C., to work at the National Museum of Natural History after graduation. She has curly dark brown hair. She is fascinated with pearls, especially the Hope Pearl, and she visits the Hope Pearl display every day. She was working at the museum on February 13, 2008. Duct tape brand C was found in her home.

4. Star Sanders was born in Panama City, Florida, where she has lived her whole life. She graduated from high school and attends the University of Georgia, where she is studying Marine Biology. She has short curly red hair. Her father is serving time in prison for stealing a pearl necklace that he intended to give her on her birthday. She has always wanted a pearl necklace, and she has always loved pearls. She last visited the National Museum of Natural History on February 13, 2008, to see the Hope Pearl. Duct tape brand D was found in her home.

On day four, a letter will be delivered to the class containing the alibis of the four suspects. The students will add this information to their suspect information sheets. One person will be eliminated as a suspect.

Suspects' Alibis

1. Sandy Shipley said that she was a visitor of the National Museum of Natural History during the day of February 13, 2008, but

she attended a meeting as chapter president in Washington, D.C. of the Rare Gem and Pearl Association. She sat at a table with five other chapter presidents, and the meeting was over at 11:00 PM.

2. Shelly Boatwright had to go back to the hotel after visiting the National Museum of Natural History on February 13, 2008, during the evening, and was sick in bed for the rest of the evening. No one saw her after she got back to the hotel.

3. Pearl Driftwood worked on February 13, 2008, until 6:00 PM, at the National Museum of Natural History, and went home immediately after work. No one saw her after she got off work.

4. Star Sanders was visiting Washington, D.C., with friends from college, but she visited the National Museum of Natural History by herself. She left the museum at 6:30 PM, and she went back to the hotel by herself. She was alone the rest of the night.

Sandy Shipley was the only suspect who had a credible alibi because she attended a meeting with five other chapter presidents during the evening of February 13, 2008. She can be eliminated through deductive reasoning as a suspect because she had witnesses who saw her at the meeting until 11:00 PM. She couldn't have committed the crime. Shelly Boatwright, Pearl Driftwood, and Star Sanders didn't have credible alibis that could be proven true by witnesses, so they remain suspects.

On day five, the first evidence packet arrives and the students work in groups using magnifying glasses and dissecting scopes or hand-held lighted scopes to closely observe the evidence. The evidence packet contains sand samples from the homes of the four suspects: Panama City Beach, Florida; Jacksonville Beach, Florida; Myrtle Beach, South Carolina; and San Salvador Island, Bahamas. There will be two sand samples from each location, which will total eight sand samples. (Sand samples will be made ahead by smearing a small amount of white school glue onto a plastic slide. Sand is then sprinkled onto the glue, and the sand will set when the glue dries.) The latitude and the longitude will be written on the slide pairs, with the latitude on one slide of the pair and the longitude on the other slide of the pair. For example: Panama City, Florida—Slide One will read 30.20 degrees latitude, and Slide Two will read 85.68 degrees longitude.

The students will use world maps to locate the latitude and longitude of each slide pair so the sand samples can be matched to a location. Sand taken from the crime scene will also be included in the evidence packet, and it will be given to the groups once the locations have been determined. The students will closely examine the sand from the crime scene and match it to one of the pairs of sand samples. The students will use deductive reasoning to eliminate two of the three remaining suspects based on the sand found at the crime scene. (The students should determine that the sand sample from the crime scene came from Panama City Beach, Florida.) They will also examine other evidence from evidence packets two and three before they solve the case.

Evidence packet two will arrive on day six, and it will contain the duct tape found at the crime scene as well as the four rolls of duct tape found in the four suspects' homes. The students will examine the edges of the duct tape found at the crime scene using magnifying glasses and dissecting microscopes or lighted hand-held plastic scopes. The groups will make notes as they examine the tape. Next, the groups will cut a one-half-inch strip of duct tape from the end of each roll and mount it onto a plastic slide so the edge can be viewed under the scopes and with magnifying glasses. The students will use deductive reasoning to identify the brand of duct tape used at the crime scene (duct tape A, B, C, or D), and then the duct tape brand will be matched to a suspect using the suspect information sheet. (The duct tape used on the security guard was duct tape brand D.) This clue should help build the case when you add it to the sand evidence.

The third evidence packet will arrive on day seven, and it will contain one hair sample found at the crime scene. This will be the final piece of evidence, and it will be matched to the person responsible for the crime. The type and color of hair found at the crime scene was short, curly, and red. The evidence proves that Star Sanders stole the Hope Pearl from the National Museum of Natural History on February 13, 2008. Case Closed!

The groups will spend day eight writing their reports that will be "mailed" to the director, and he will send them a certificate of appreciation several days later for their excellent forensic investigative work.

HelpfulTips

I have found that the time involved in creating mystery crime units is more than worth the effort. My students can't wait for the next opportunity to solve a mystery. I have found that younger students work best with three to four suspects and three to four clues for each crime. Older students need six to seven suspects and six to seven clues to allow more investigative opportunities. The crimes can involve the theft of animals of great value as well as the theft of expensive items such as art, cars, gems, rare coins, and so on. Evidence can be crumbs, tape, hair, sand, plant matter, blood, fingerprints, footprints, tire tread, unknown powders, and so on. Be creative, and have a good time writing your mysteries!

20. Journey With the Loggerheads

Nancy Bryant
Supply, North Carolina

Recommended Level: Grades 2–5+

Overall Objective: To actively engage students in learning about sea turtles and ecosystems. This multidisciplinary unit also involves technology, math, literature, art, field trips, and community service.

Standards Met (North Carolina):

English Language Arts: Read independently from selected materials; Apply strategies and skills to comprehend text that is read and heard; Listen actively and critically and make connections through written language, media, and technology

Math: Understand and use graphs; Use standard units of metric and customary measurement; Compute whole numbers and recognize and use basic geometric properties of two- and three-dimensional figures

Science: Make observations and conduct investigations to build an understanding of animal behavior and adaptation; Build an understanding of the interdependence of plants and animals

Social Studies: Apply geographical themes of NC; Evaluate human-environmental interactions and impacts

Materials Needed:

- Internet Web sites: https://www.cccturtle.org/Secure/ed_pdf.php; http://www.oceanconservancy.org/site/DocServer?docID=481; http://www.seaturtlehospital.org/; http://139.70.40.46/loggrhd.htm
- Video: *Tales From the Wild: Cara the Sea Turtle* (Wilk, 1998)
- Video: *The Living Sea* (MacGillivray, 1995)
- Art supplies for sea mural (glue sticks, construction paper, tennis balls for sea turtle eggs, markers, and bulletin board paper)
- Art supplies for turtle puppets available at http://www.sandiegozoo.org/kids/craft_trash_puppet.html
- PowerPoint, Microsoft Publisher, and access to computers
- Turtle poetry taken from various Web sites
- Guest speakers from Sea Turtle Patrol and local museums
- Digital cameras
- *Turtle Bay* by Saviour Pirotta (1997)

Since I live in the coastal region of southeast North Carolina, I decided to create a unit to teach students about the loggerhead sea turtle. This unit allowed students from different grade levels (in this case, third through fifth graders) to explore, research, and learn not only about our native turtles but also about our coastal and ocean ecosystems, conservation, community service, recycling, literature, poetry writing, math, and technology. As a result of the many hands-on activities, real-life learning, and the implementation of technology, the students were actively engaged throughout the entire unit. In addition, the students were able to participate in activities that created excitement for learning!

To begin the unit, students read the short story *Turtle Bay* (Pirotta, 1997). The classes then discussed the story, focusing on sea turtles' nesting habits and how humans can help sea turtles. Then, the loggerhead sea turtle was introduced using the video *Tales From the Wild: Cara the Sea Turtle* (Wilk, 1998) and a guest speaker from the local coastal museum and sea turtle patrol.

During the next week, students read the teacher-made booklets and answered related comprehension questions and the book *Sea Turtles* (Jacobs, 2003) printed from the Internet. In these booklets, students applied math and reading skills to answer questions such as comprehension and converting metric to customary measurements (using the Web site http://www.metric-conversions.org/measurement-conversions .htm). In addition, students determined and discussed why the loggerhead is an endangered species. They researched other animals on the endangered species list via the Internet and listed causes of the species becoming endangered. Students then brainstormed ideas on how to help the loggerhead sea turtles. Students then each selected a specific sea turtle and created a scale-sized drawings of them using graph paper. By the end of the week, students were able to identify the seven types of sea turtles, explain a sea turtle's life cycle, describe a sea turtle's habitat and ecosystem, and discuss ideas on how to help the sea turtles survive.

At the beginning of the third week, students were given digital cameras and transported to a local coastal museum to experience hands-on learning about our coastal environment and the loggerheads. The students were instructed to use the digital cameras to take pictures of their learning at the museum. They were informed that the pictures they took would be used in the PowerPoint presentation that they would create. Students also used these cameras to document their work on our "Sea Life Hall." The students created two- and three-dimensional sea turtles and other sea life and displayed it in the school's hall. Walking down the hall felt like you were actually walking under the ocean's surface! The students also created a beach scene, depicting loggerhead hatchlings going to the ocean from their nest in the sand dunes, and they made a wall informing students how trash negatively affects turtles. To get support from the entire school, each class was invited to make their own sea art and put it in the hall. Also, a Sea Life Poetry contest was held for every student to enter.

During the final week, students traveled to Topsail Beach, North Carolina, to help the Karen Beasley Sea Turtle Hospital release 20 sea turtles! Again, digital cameras were used to capture this special moment. Students also increased their community service by raising money for the hospital. Their fundraiser, "A Dollar for a Logger," raised over $200.00. Back at school, students worked and completed their PowerPoint presentations and created sea turtle puppets using trash (for examples, see http://www.sandiegozoo.org/kids/craft_trash_puppet.html). As a culminating event, the students invited their families to Seafood Festival night at Supply Elementary. Students created invitations using Microsoft Publisher for this event. On this special night, students presented their PowerPoint to their families, and everyone enjoyed local seafood for dinner!

References

Jacobs, F. (2003). *Sea turtles.* Washington, DC: The Ocean Conservancy. Retrieved April 6, 2009, from http://www.oceanconservancy.org/site/DocServer?docID=481

MacGillivray, G. (Director), Holzberg, R., & Cahill, T. (Writers). (1995). *The living sea.* New Orleans, LA: Aquarium of the Americas.

Pirotta, S. (1997). *Turtle Bay.* New York: Farrar, Straus, and Giroux.

Wilk, A. C. (1998). *From the wild: Cara the sea turtle* [Motion picture]. Questar Video.

ℝ   21. Inquiry and Integration

Amy Nicholl
Windsor, Colorado

Recommended Level: Grades 3–5

Overall Objective: To get kids interested in science through guided and open inquiry and to make time to teach science by integrating it with other subject areas.

Science is taught almost daily in my class. In fact, the students literally groan on any day when science is pushed off the plate. When I share this with other teachers, they always ask me how I can have time to teach science that many times a week. Like other elementary teachers, I am responsible to teach all of the subject areas and am responsible for preparing my students for the state test in the spring. I have time to teach it because I look for those areas where I can overlap the standards. By teaching math skills such as graphing, data tables, averaging, and interpreting data through science experiments, my class can usually skim over that chapter in our textbook.

The Learning Cycle Guided Inquiry:

Many years ago, I was introduced to the learning cycle method (or the 5 Es) by Dr. Jay Hackett (Moyer, Hackett, & Everett, 2006) as a way to teach science effectively. It has been such a part of my teaching since then that I use it in all subject areas. The 5 Es include engage, explore, explain, elaborate/apply, and evaluate/assess.

Engage

To model this type of integration, let's stroll through a unit on motion. To *engage* the students, I set up a discrepant event in the front of my room. I stack a jar of water, a piece of cardboard, an empty toilet paper roll, and an egg. I ask the students, "How can I get the egg into the water." With wide eyes, thinking I'm crazy, they may say something like, "Well, pick up the egg, move the other stuff and drop it into the water!" I have to admit, that is obviously a great answer, but I want them to keep thinking so—I say, "Well, that would work, but I can't touch it. Now, what do you think I should do?" I tell the students to write their ideas or draw them in their science notebooks. A few more students will share their ideas with me and then I saunter over to the side of the room where a broom from my house just happens to be leaning. I usually hold it similar to preparing to hit a home run and then ask, "What do you think? Should I give it a whack?" It is so fun to be a teacher, watching the students' faces as they lean closer trying to figure out if I would really hit it like a baseball slugger. Taking the broom in my hands, I place my foot firmly on the bristles and pull it back so that when released, the handle of the broom will hit the cardboard that is sitting slightly over the table. The kids give a drum roll on their legs while we do a countdown, "5, 4, 3, 2 . . . 1." The broom handle is released and hits the cardboard. The cardboard piece goes flying, the toilet paper roll tilts, and with a nice "kerplunk," the egg falls into the water.

Explore

After the "oohs" and "ahhs" have subsided, I explain to them that they will be doing experiments to help explain what was happening in the demonstration. This is the *explore* stage of the 5 Es model. Prior to the class, I organize gift bags with the materials and directions the students will use for their experiments, an idea that I gleaned from my teaching partner, Teri Romshek. These materials include dominoes, pennies, stacking cups, and waxed paper with a jar. All of the experiments model for the students the concept of inertia or Newton's first law of motion. The groups have about ten minutes to work through each bag, and then they place everything back into the bags and rotate them to the next group. This is a great way to manage materials and efficiently gets the students through multiple experiments. It is extremely important for the students to be able to manipulate the materials and experience the concept. For each bag or experiment, the students are responsible for recording their observations and thoughts into their science notebooks.

Explain

After the students experiment, we come back together as a class. Through questioning the students, I pull out the important concepts that I want them to learn through their experience. The *explain* stage builds the science concept by using observations during the experiment to help students explain the science concept I want them to learn. In this example, the activities during the experiment teach the concept of inertia.

Elaborate/Apply

The next phase is to *elaborate* or *apply* their learning to the world around them. Students who have the opportunity to learn through this inquiry model become amazing observers of the world around them. They begin to see "science" everywhere. During this lesson, the students are asked where they have observed similar events involving inertia. These may include a magician pulling the tablecloth out from under a set of dishes, their bicycles continuing to roll down a hill, or why we need to wear seatbelts.

Evaluate/Assess

To *evaluate* or *assess* the students learning, they may be asked to write a short summary of what they learned, or write their explanation for what happened in the engage phase (the egg over the water) using the terms that they learned during the class. Sometimes my students will write a short summary, where each word costs ten cents and they must write their summary using enough words to get as close to two dollars as possible without going over that amount.

We wrap up this lesson by having a volunteer come to the front of the room and repeat the engage activity. The class has a blast watching the egg go splashing into the water again. Many students go home that night excited about science and asking their parents for just one egg!

This is an example of a guided-inquiry lesson. Although the students were allowed to experiment and help develop the concept, the teacher guided the experiment. Sometimes this is the best approach to meet the learning objectives that I need to cover, but I also want my students to learn how to design their own experiments. Early in the year, my students experiment with a variety of materials from getting "poppers" to pop on their own, to discovering what happens when milk dotted with food coloring is touched by a toothpick covered in soap. During both of these activities, students are encouraged to make observations and ask "I wonder" questions. These questions include things like "I wonder why the poppers are made from rubber?" "I wonder what would happen if we heated one popper and placed another popper in the refrigerator?" "I wonder what would happen if we placed the food coloring and soap in 1% milk or heavy cream?"

After the students have done some of these types of experiments, we discuss as a class what questions are researchable and which ones are testable. The students soon learn that the questions containing *why* are usually best for research while the questions that ask *what would happen if* are great for testing. These activities encourage the students to always ask questions and always seek answers to those questions. In other words, the students begin to think. As educators, this should be what we strive for in our classrooms. My students begin to carry this "I wonder" mentality into the whole day! "I wonder why the character in our novel would act that way." "I wonder why the authors choose those words to describe the forest." This feeling of wonder is a magical phenomenon in a classroom.

Moving to Open Inquiry

During another part of the motion unit, I show the students a film canister and Alka Seltzer tablets and tell them that they will be designing Alka Seltzer rockets. The students work in groups to brainstorm all of the variables that they could test, and they write their ideas on sticky notes (one variable on each note). Ideas include trying different amounts of water, different temperatures of water, different amounts of the tablets, different angles of release, and so on. In their groups, the students then choose one variable that they would like to test. All of the rest of the variables are placed off to the side and must be kept the same during the experiment. Then the groups discuss what they could measure, and they write these ideas on differently colored sticky notes. These ideas might include the distance the canister travels, how long it takes for the canister to pop, or how high it travels. The groups choose one of these ideas and then come up with a testable question that they would like to explore. Students think through the following steps: From our question, what do we want to modify or change? (This is the independent variable.) What will stay the same? (These are controlled variables.) What will we measure or observe? From these questions, the students determine their procedure and what materials they will need to conduct their experiment. As a group, we also discuss safety issues, such as the use of safety goggles and why leaning directly over the film canister containing the Alka Seltzer tablet and water would be a really bad idea.

Once the students have chosen the variable that they wish to test and decided how they will test it, they make their predictions. I encourage the students to write their predictions describing what they think will happen and then give a reason to support their thinking. While they are conducting their experiment, the students create their own data table and graph their results. During this time, students are using their math skills to measure in centimeters or seconds, record their data, average their results, and graph the averages. The students will then use their data and graphs to draw conclusions. In their conclusions, students are expected to compare their prediction with their results, describe their results, and give specific evidence from their data to support their findings. Students are also encouraged to come up with new questions, new "I wonders." Some of these can be investigated further and others can be researched, and the information they produced can be shared with the rest of the class.

Science Notebooks

In 2006, I was able to go to a workshop with Dr. Michael Klentschy (2006) on the topic of increasing student learning through science and literacy connections. Science notebooks provide a key to integrating literacy with science by allowing students to process their learning through words and illustrations. Science notebooks have become a vital tool in my classroom. This tool provides students a place to record their thinking and their learning before, during, and after a science investigation. It is a place for students to record their observations in both writing and technical drawing. Throughout the year, the science notebook also allows them to see the growth in their understanding of scientific concepts. These notebooks are constructed like a science text. The students create a title page for their units, a table, and a glossary. The pride that students have in their notebooks has been amazing. When we begin our notebooks in the fall, I share examples of science notebooks and nature journals from people like Lewis and Clark to Thomas Edison. After the students look at these examples, we discuss the difference between the types of technical drawings needed for science compared to the illustrations that they may draw in art.

Integrating Writing

In the area of writing, I save time by applying the skills we are learning in writing to the content we are learning in science. After teaching writing organized paragraphs, the students apply what they know to writing expository paragraphs and essays on science topics. For example, during the motion unit described earlier, the students have the opportunity to go bowling. During our bowling field trip, the students see Newton's laws up close and personal. They get to bowl in their socks and can feel Newton's third law as they slide backwards after releasing the ball. They see how changing the amount of friction changes how quickly the ball rolls as they try it on the carpet and rolling it down the lane. By taking the kids behind the lanes, they can see how gravity is used to return the balls back to the bowlers. After this experience, the students come back and write an expository essay about their experience. They are required to use science terminology covered in science class as well as literary devices we've covered in language arts classes. These include onomatopoeia, similes, metaphors, alliteration, and strong verbs. Their expository paragraphs are also organized according to what they have learned in class, with topic sentences, transitions, and conclusions.

For narrative practice, the students read an informational text about Sir Isaac Newton. Then, using some of the facts that they learned from their study, they create a fictional tale about how Newton might have "really" come up with his laws. For example, perhaps Isaac Newton was resting one day from his labor on the farm and sat under a tree to rest. Looking toward the top of a hill he notices a cart that is just resting where someone left it. The next day, he returns to the same spot and looks again toward the hill. "Ah, ha . . . a cart at rest must stay at rest until something comes along and moves it!" This might have been how he discovered the first part of his first law! Who knows? By doing this activity, the students' creative juices start flowing. They not only are learning about elements of a story—setting, characters, and plot—but they are also having a great time trying to figure out what Sir Isaac Newton could have been doing when he found out about each of his laws. They are applying their science understanding of motion to their creation of a wonderful story.

A short writing activity is *3 . . . 2 . . . 1*. This activity can be used at the end of an investigation: Students write three facts they've learned, two terms they want to remember, and one question they have.

Integrating Reading

During this unit, students also have opportunity to read through various nonfiction books. I ask students to notice any differences between books and the novels that we are reading in class. In their groups, they make a Venn diagram of the similarities and differences between informational and narrative text structures. Things that were highlighted included the use of the table of contents, glossary, index, picture captions, and highlighted words. I could have done the same lesson during my literacy block by handing out a worksheet from the series that covered these concepts, but it was much more meaningful to have the students discover this literacy standard in the context of the content we were learning.

In reading, we want students to question, predict, compare, and contrast. We ask the students to infer, draw conclusions, and to support their answers with evidence from the text. Students are taught how to make connections, make mental pictures, and determine the importance of text. All of these strategies we want our students to apply to reading can be done through informational text that supports what the students are studying in science as well as in their reading novels or textbooks.

Main Idea

To help students understand the main idea of the material they read, give each student 10 sticky notes. As they read the material, they can jot down a word that they think is important in understanding the concept. Each important word is written on its own sticky note. Students can change their mind as they read through the text and pick a different word. At the end of their reading, they post their 10 "most important" words on the board. Draw a line on the board and ask the students to post their words one or two students at a time. If a student has a word that is already on the line, they place it above the other person's sticky note. By the time the class has finished, they should notice that some words have many sticky notes. Discuss with the students why some of these words have been posted more frequently than others. Students will discover that the main idea of the passage is reflected by the words written most frequently. Students can use this activity to write a summary of their reading material.

Another idea for helping students find the main ideas while reading through informational texts is to give them sticky notes; then, as the students read, they record one main thought per page of their reading material. When they are finished reading, they can go back and review the sticky notes to prepare for a classroom discussion or a written summary.

Word Walls

To increase the vocabulary of students, word walls can be very effective. Not only having the word listed but also allowing the students to illustrate the meaning of the word or having a sample of the word is very helpful for the students. Students can refer to these words throughout the unit.

Vocabulary Instruction

The Frayer Model is an effective way for students to grasp new terms.

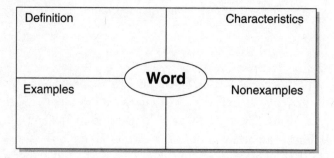

Pair Two: At the beginning of a unit or before reading informational text, the teacher can write a variety of terms that will be used on the board in two columns. The teacher then instructs the students to pair up a set of words that they think can be connected in some way. The students state the pairs and give their reasons for the connection.

These are just a few of the ideas that I use throughout the year to entwine my content with the tools needed to understand the content (reading, writing, and math). I have a poster in my room that states, "The more I know, the more I know that there is so much more to know." This is so true about effective teaching. I know that to be an effective teacher, even after 29 years in the classroom, I need to constantly be reading, learning, and changing.

The ocean is a vast place filled with an incredible array of life, and always changing. Sounds a lot like teaching! Let's just remember to keep the fish and the water in the same bowl.

References

Klentschy, M. (2006, November). NSTA Research Dissemination Conference, Baltimore, MD.
Moyer, R. H., Hackett, J. K., & Everett, S. A. (2006). *Teaching science as investigations: Modeling inquiry through learning cycle lessons.* Upper Saddle River, NJ: Prentice Hall.

22. Scientific Investigations Driven by "Inquiry"

Debbie Easley
Somerville, Alabama

Recommended Level: Grade 5

Overall Objective: Students will practice the steps of an investigation using guided and independent inquiry, while realizing the significance and implications of using a science journal as a scientific tool.

Standards Met (Alabama):

Science: Identify evidence of chemical changes through color, gas formation, solid formation, and temperature change; Relate density to the sinking or floating of an object; Contrast ways in which light rays are bent by concave and convex lenses; Identify questions that can be answered through scientific investigations; Design and conduct a scientific investigation; Use appropriate tools and techniques to gather, analyze and interpret data

Materials Needed:

- Chart and markers
- **Station 1**—colored pencils, flashlights, golf tees
- **Station 2**—cups, vinegar, baking soda, paper towels, dump station
- **Station 3**—basin with water, aluminum foil, pennies, paper towels
- **Station 4**—electric microscope, manual microscope, prepared slides, student journal, pencil
- **Station 5**—cup with carbonated drink, raisins

Note: Each station requires student journal and pencil

Lesson Development

Procedure: The 5 E-learning Cycle (Moyer, Hackett, & Everett, 2006) is the most efficient means for achieving a risk-free learning environment and meeting my objectives. This strategy supports inquiry learning and triggers students' natural curiosity. The 5 Es are engagement, exploration, explanation, evaluation, and extension.

Engagement: To set the stage for interest and excitement, I dim the lights and use the flashlight to maneuver the shadow of a pencil. The room becomes abuzz with excitement.

Exploration: Students are then given flashlights and golf tees and asked to "explore" the relationship between light and shadow. I remind them to use their journals to record data. During their free exploration, I circulate about the room observing and noting any questions I overhear. After about five minutes, I ask, "What investigations did you conduct? Did any questions come up?" Their responses are recorded on my classroom content/inquiry chart. I'll spotlight the scientific model and ask if anyone used any part of it during their free exploration. It's important to lead students to identify for themselves where they have used the process. Any parts of the scientific process mentioned are highlighted on the chart. Logistical instructions are given verbally as well displayed on the overhead. This includes time allotments, proper movement from station to station, expected "scientific" behavior, and use of their science journal. Eight minutes per station is allowed. Preassigned groups of students move about the room from station to station working through the investigations. I begin with station one and circulate about the room during station time. I remind students that, due to time constraints, they will not be able to visit each station, but each station's results will be shared in the large group.

Explanation: After students have had the opportunity to visit three of the five stations, I call the groups back to their original positions. While each group shares findings, I write down any mention of the components of a scientific investigation on chart paper and compare their responses to the steps in a scientific investigation. Similarities between the two are emphasized, and time is spent reinforcing the importance of using the steps to record their investigation.

Evaluation: Informal assessment goes on from the onset of this investigative lesson and is supported by a self-evaluation performed by students. They use a rubric to score themselves. These assessments are valuable snapshots into the child's thinking and how they perceive themselves as scientists. Next, I take up their individual journals and use the same rubric to assess student work and my own instruction. Usually, it's very clear which way I need to go from here and who needs a little more of my personal attention.

Extension: This arm of the learning cycle encourages students to stretch their thinking and wonder "what if." I ask them to revisit any new questions they might have had during the inquiry time. Unfortunately, time constraints often hinder much further in-class investigation, but I always strongly suggest they take their interests further by investigating at home if at all possible. I am always amazed at the interest that blossoms and the excited oral reports that come in the days that follow.

Helpful Tips

- When conducting inquiry learning, always be prepared for the next new question and where it might take you. I try to keep my cabinets full of odds and ends that will serve as components of an inquiry.
- Careful management of time and behavior is essential. Without it, your "ordered chaos" will quickly get out of hand and you'll find yourself dreading your next science lesson. I use colored poker chips to manage my groups. The white chip is worth 100 points, the blue is 50 points, and the red is a negative 5. With group charts posted and classroom jobs of chip collector and recorder, this management tool works efficiently with little extra effort on my part. The highest chip score is rewarded with pizza and a drink every five to six weeks. I also use something called the "observer's clipboard." This is promptly handed to someone who is having difficulty thinking "scientifically" during the science lesson. The misbehavior is rewarded with the clipboard and they are asked to join another group where they will have the arduous task of observing only. No hands-on for them. I have to say, since I've instituted the clipboard, I've only had to use it once or twice. Students really want to be involved and handle the equipment.
- Journal management is tricky if you teach more than one section of science or more than 24 students, which, the last time I checked, is the rule now instead of the exception. If you don't take a personal interest in each journal and respond to at least some of the entries, students will clearly see that the journal's importance is nonexistent. In order to work my way through my mountain of journals, I color code the journals and make management a snap. By assigning four to five different colors to the class, I'm able to set "color deadlines" and take up as few as six to seven journals at a time. It sure makes checking less stressful and responding a reality. Students love to read my responses, and I gain rich insight into the thinking, strengths, and concerns of my students.

What does all this inquiry teaching gain for me and my students? Well, right now, I see a height of interest and enthusiasm that continues to amaze me. I see students who once "hated" science carrying their journals to break "just in case they find something to investigate." I witness students asking questions and making inquiries into subjects that I only considered when I was in high school, and believe me, even then they were quite limited. I hear conversations using vocabulary that I know will arm them for future testing and scientific experiences. This one is special. I have visits, e-mails, and lovely notes from junior and senior high students who still have a love and desire to investigate and learn more about scientific phenomenon.

Will I ever teach using another method? Well, I'm always open to suggestions, but it is beyond me that inquiry learning will ever be replaced with another more effective means of gaining scientific experience. Besides, it's the most fun I have all day!

Reference

Moyer, R. H., Hackett, J. K., & Everett, S. A. (2006). *Teaching science as investigations: Modeling inquiry through learning cycle lessons*. Upper Saddle River, NJ: Prentice Hall.

Teaching Math

Overview, Chapters 23–30

23. **Lisa M. Hall,** a mathematics specialist in Richmond, Virginia, creates schoolwide math motivators that are implemented throughout her entire elementary school. Students get excited about learning math as they compete against each other to win weekly and monthly prizes.

24. **Barb A. Egbert,** a kindergarten teacher from Cape Girardeau, Missouri, teaches her kindergartners about two- and three-dimensional figures using building blocks the kids love to play with. Depending on skill level, students will verbalize or otherwise demonstrate their newfound knowledge of geometric relationships.

25. **Ganna Maymind,** a first-grade teacher from Morganville, New Jersey, uses popular children's literature to teach students about coin counting. Working together, the students learn how much coins are worth and practice adding value. They conclude the lesson by writing their own story about coins.

26. **Deb Guthrie,** a second-grade teacher from Arden Hills, Minnesota, teaches triangles by having her students build shapes using toothpicks. The students also learn about patterns as they see how the number of toothpicks increases when triangles are stacked side by side.

27. **Kelli Higgins,** a third-grade teacher from Illinois, holds a school-wide math-a-thon to get students geared up for statewide testing and to reinforce math practices. Students can refresh their memories and prepare for testing in a stress-free climate.

28. **Debbie Gordon,** a third-grade teacher from Arizona, uses a popular children's book, *Stacks of Trouble,* to differentiate multiplication problem solving to meet the individual needs of the students in her math classroom. Students use whiteboards to solve the problems embedded in the book.

29. **Pam Cyr**, a fifth-grade teacher from Vermont, shows students how to describe and classify triangles and quadrilaterals. Pam uses non-examples as a key method for explaining what triangles are, and students get hands-on experience building shapes using polystrips.

30. **Shari Kaneshiro,** a fifth-grade teacher from Hawaii, encourages her fifth-grade students use their critical-thinking, problem-solving, and mathematical skills to help with their school's annual fundraiser. In this service-learning project, students apply knowledge of circumference to measure out the track for the school's fun run.

23. Schoolwide Math Motivators

Lisa M. Hall
Richmond, Virginia

Recommended Level: Grades K–5

Overall Objective: To foster excitement and enthusiasm for learning mathematics.

Standards Met (Virginia):

Number Sense; Basic Fact Mastery; Estimation; Mathematical Communication

Materials Needed: See descriptions below. Each activity requires motivational rewards, such as fancy pencils erasers and award ribbons.

Today's schools are competing with a world of video games, reality TV, and instant gratification. It seems that today's teachers need a gimmick, something to draw their students in and keep their attention. Teachers now need to find innovative, entertaining activities to excite children about learning and make it relevant in their lives.

As a Title I mathematics specialist in an at-risk elementary school, I have been collecting ideas and creating programs designed to motivate the whole school population, kindergarten through fifth grade, in mathematics. Unlike traditional classroom mathematics instruction, where the classroom teacher teaches a lesson to a self-contained group of 20 children, schoolwide activities allow an *entire school of students* to participate in learning activities together. This creates a learning community where everyone shares in the same thinking, experiences, and excitement. Opportunities for listening skills, mathematical communication, vocabulary development, and real-world applications of mathematics are available to all grades of students simultaneously. Self-esteem and pride in learning mathematics are fostered schoolwide as students hear their names stated during announcements, receive awards, and receive special invitations to schoolwide celebrations. Here are some activities that have excited my students about learning mathematics throughout my school building.

Guessing Jars: Each month, two Guessing Jars (one jar for Grades K–2 and another for Grades 3–5) are passed from classroom to classroom. These jars are filled with items such as M&M's, mini candy bars, or wrapped taffy. Students in each class write down their estimates of the number of items inside the jar on a Guessing Jar slip. At the end of the month, after the jars have visited every class, students in each grade level with the closest estimate are recognized as Guessing Jar winners and receive special prizes, such as a checkers game or an art set. These estimators are also recognized in the daily announcements.

I try to vary the estimation task on occasion. For example, during the measurement unit for fourth and fifth grade, I found the mass of one piece of taffy to be 8 grams. The task for the students was to estimate the mass of all the pieces of taffy in the Guessing Jar. Not only did students need to think about how many pieces were in the jar, but they also used problem-solving strategies and operations to calculate mass. In this activity, students were provided with a *reason* to compute.

Math Fact of the Week: Each Monday morning, the "Math Fact of the Week" is announced in the daily announcements. One fact for kindergarten through second grade, such as $4 + 5$, and one fact for third through fifth grade, such as 7×8, is announced. Students have the opportunity to place their answers to the Math Fact of the Week in the answer jar in the front office. On Friday, one correct kindergarten through second-grade answer and one correct third- through fifth-grade answer are drawn from the jar, and those students win a small prize, such as a fancy pencil or eraser, and recognition during the announcements. Facts can include basic facts as well as mathematical facts, such as "What is a triangle with only two equivalent sides called?"

Students and teachers alike have come to look forward to hearing these questions each morning and can't wait to submit their answers in the answer jar. Friday mornings are exciting, as students listen intently for the answer to the week's math question and hope to hear their names announced as winners. This has been a very motivating event during morning announcements.

Math Maestros: Each month, students at every grade level can participate in the "Math Challenge," a performance task to assess students' conceptual understanding of basic math concepts. For example, third- and fourth-grade students might be presented with a basic fact or idea, such as 4×7, and asked to represent their answers in pictures, numbers, and words. A different Math Challenge is created for each grade level every month. Students who can successfully complete these performance tasks are recognized on announcements as Math Maestros and are invited to join in the monthly Math Maestros celebration. These celebrations vary monthly based on holidays and seasons and might include ice cream or pizza parties, bubble blowing contests, dances, and games.

Math Poster Contests: During Math Month, students are asked to design posters that depict important mathematical ideas appropriate for their grade levels, such as how to find area for fifth grade or how to measure the length of a turtle using bean counters in first grade. These posters are displayed around the school hallways all month. Posters are judged on accuracy and creativity. One poster from each grade level is selected to be framed and displayed in a special place in the school as the grade-level winner. Just imagine your school hallways covered in mathematics—it's a beautiful site to see!

"Mathwear" Parade: Students decorate clothing, such as plain white T-shirts or hats, with math ideas. They can use fabric paints, but permanent markers are less costly and work well to decorate cloth. Some teachers have been very creative and helped their students design jewelry, vests, and crazy hats with math facts and vocabulary. For my mathwear outfit, I purchased an inexpensive pair of dark blue nurse's scrubs and a bottle of fabric paint from Wal-Mart; I decorated my scrubs with multiplication facts, math words, and geometric shapes. I attract much attention as I strut around the school in my math scrubs!

On Math Day, all students are asked to wear their creations. In the afternoon, festive music is played on the intercom as each grade level has an opportunity to march the hallways. The most spirited and creative classrooms from each grade level win three-foot sub parties, and they must use math to decide the best way to divide the sandwich equally among all students in the class.

Support for Schoolwide Activities

Many of the programs I have implemented have been funded with grants from local and national organizations. Education foundations, power companies, financial organizations, and local vendors are very generous in their support of programs to help challenged schools. In addition to grants, many school PTAs or PTOs have money set aside for school projects and would be especially willing to support schoolwide learning programs. Without the support of these groups, many of the activities I have organized for our school would not have been as effective in motivating our students.

Schoolwide learning activities help boost morale and add spark to the regular school day. Students take pride and ownership of learning when they can be recognized for working hard. Most important, these activities have brought fun back into the school setting.

24. Differentiation in Kindergarten Geometry

Barb A. Egbert
Cape Girardeau, Missouri

Recommended Level: Kindergarten

Overall Objective: To introduce students to two- and three-dimensional shapes.

Materials Needed: Materials used in this investigation include center signs for each activity, with activity name, the steps to the activity, a picture that illustrates for the nonreader the general idea of the activity, and materials required. On the back, there are questions to help the educator, assistant, or volunteer assist the child in discussing his thought process. We use Geoblocks, a set of blocks that are cut to specific dimensions, calibrated to configure small blocks to compose a larger block in the same set. Mats with corresponding 2-D face shapes are copied on card stock and laminated. In addition, Pattern Blocks are utilized, with card stock laminated mats that have six hexagon outlines. Finally, we use a virtual manipulative computer program, Scott Foresman's *Shapes* software, which allows children to manipulate pattern block shapes on a vertical surface through the use of a mouse.

There are several opportunities to investigate the standard, using a variety of resources (Investigations has excellent learning and coaching activities, through instructional/named centers). Build a Block requires seeing a 3-D shape's attributes and reproducing it with smaller blocks. Matching Faces necessitates recognition and comparison of 3-D block parts. Geoblock Match-Up requires face shape detection and matching 2-D game board shapes. Fill the Hexagon uses 2-D Pattern Blocks to fill game board outlines. Pattern Block Puzzles require horizontal (blocks and mats) and vertical (Scott Foresman's *Shapes* computer software) formats. The children choose what and whom they will work with to discover more about shape names and attributes. A great deal of modeling and copying goes on, but the teacher's job is to get the children talking about their thinking.

Before the Lesson

Prior to the lesson, there is much exploring in geometry. Pattern Blocks and Geoblocks are always accessible for student-directed and teacher-directed investigations. Trade books model verbalization and visualization of shapes and begin conversations in finding 2-D and 3-D shapes in the classroom, on campus, and at home. Early class projects include a *Shapes* class book and murals using Pattern Block shapes. 2-D and 3-D shapes are discussed, named, modeled, constructed with clay, and utilized to create and copy designs. Geoboards are introduced prior to this lesson. Recording is stressed to improve the ability to get thought onto paper and share ideas. The computer is utilized through the *Shapes* software, using Pattern Block shapes to organize an original picture and fill a predetermined outline (composing and decomposing shapes). An activity called Quick Images is explored, in which spatial memory is used to replicate a briefly flashed block image. We move from child-driven exploration of shapes, through group projects to aid in all children contributing, to less concrete, more curriculum-driven investigations. Centers are introduced to the class, and then performance is observed by the teacher (reducing or enhancing tasks to fit individuals).

There is a wide range of understanding prior to this lesson. Most of the children are able to recognize, name, compare, and sort 2-D shapes; a few still show signs of confusing the rectangle and triangle names. Many are able to discuss similarities or differences in 2-D shape attributes, using their own language, but more work is needed for all children to be able to talk about 3-D shapes. Some children have begun to predict the results of composing and decomposing Pattern Block shapes; 3-D shapes need teacher-direction. There is much confusion between the formal names of 2- and 3-D shapes; this will be an ongoing topic in future school and home newsletters. Most children are able to replicate a pictured design with Pattern Blocks. Some children notice that in order to have matching faces they need the same shape and size; more time should be paid to this skill.

Expectations

During this featured lesson, I am hoping to help some children through the rectangle/triangle confusion, because sometimes it is simply a problem of articulating the formal name. I want to assist the understanding that 2-D shapes can be found on 3-D shapes and the idea that 2-D shapes are flat (circle verses a ball or sphere). Expansion is needed on the idea that smaller shapes can make larger shapes. The main goal is to get the children to discuss and describe, in their own words, what they see related between 2-D and 3-D shapes, solving the presented challenges.

Future instruction will guide children through the following investigations: Collect ways that a hexagon could be made using Pattern Blocks (composing, decomposing, and recording 2-D shapes); collect ways to represent a given Geoblock (discussing, composing, and decomposing 3-D shapes); and try *Planning Pictures,* which asks the children to plan a Pattern Block picture on the table with blocks and then copy it to the computer screen (drawing and building and composing pictures using 2-D shape attributes). Much discussion will ensue!

It is my hope that the sequence of informal shape knowledge to more formal concept knowledge will develop strong, critical thinkers. All learners need to investigate materials and mathematical concepts through preferred styles. The standard was initially addressed through group projects, so no one felt uncomfortable about working with the shapes. However, only some children respond to large-group instruction, so most need the small-group, hands-on, individual conversations to build concepts. Multiple ways to one concept build fluency, speed, and agility—serving these future adults well!

Assessment throughout the instructional sequence is recorded by an informal checklist from the Scott Foresman Web site, breaking up the NCTM (National Council of Teachers of Mathematics) Expectations, 13 observable tasks for 2-D and eight for 3-D shapes. I've added recognizing and creating symmetrical shapes or designs. Some observations take place in large-group sessions, but mostly in small groups, asking individuals questions about work in progress or to create, name, or describe a specific task. *I use more formal performance tasks and rubrics toward the end of this instructional sequence,* observing and rating individual performances at two of the current activities. The first task rates the children on how many different ways they independently make a hexagon with Pattern Blocks. (Some children will be able to do this without an outline forming the hexagons, others need the shape to fill, and still others need one-on-one guidance by peers and the teacher. Some can achieve this by gluing paper shapes, and others require the concretely shaped blocks). The second task will give children the opportunity to show and tell what they independently know about pictured 3-D shapes by sorting and discussing blocks and real-world objects. Results will drive center activities and instruction until the end of the year and will be recorded in each child's portfolio for next year's use.

The Lesson

The introduction utilizes class discussion on prior activities regarding the geometry standard (two kinds of shapes and how they are different, small shapes making bigger shapes, formal 2-D and 3-D shape names, shape painting, describing 2-D shapes, reading shape books, and Shape Hunt), so that today's investigations are more relevant, extending knowledge of 2-D and 3-D shapes. Standard concepts are developed with activity introductions. Matching Faces shifts us into the term *faces*. In the Build a Block center, the children will create a new shape when they place two blocks adjacent, matching like faces. Often, children refer to faces as "sides," and it is my job to mention that older students call them "faces." Geoblock Match-Up makes the matching faces concept more abstract, using 2-D shapes on a game board surface. Some will understand that one block may fit more than one game board shape.

In the conclusion, we voluntarily share our discoveries of what we learned about the parts of 2-D and 3-D shapes. Some have composed shapes while others performed the simpler task of matching shapes. Many children will need guidance to find words to talk about their discoveries in future sessions. I state future goals and review how to record and share our work. I might choose to have a child who makes a cube with two triangular prisms share and verbalize how she managed this! The other children always seem to benefit by listening to their peers' explanations. I'm also sensitive to gains of particular children. Here is where informal assessment takes place—to know how to proceed with this standard in tomorrow's lesson. Are there children that need to do more investigation in a center? Or do I need to move one activity out, or increase its difficulty?

Reflections

Paraphrase response-attempts, being careful to honor the effort behind each. I don't mind repeating myself to get important points across, and I don't tire of the students' high energy. I tend to motivate with my enthusiasm and energy, always looking for different ways for the children to experience a concept.

I seem more effective if I don't jump in to communicate for the children. At a recent Missouri Staff Development Counsel Conference, one of the keynote speakers said, "Stop talking, and let the children think!" I'm attempting to keep the lesson moving by talking for them, but maybe I'm just dragging folks along! I continually attempt to use "questions that stimulate additional inquiry [to] guide further learning" (National Research Council, 2005, p. 11). Workshop time usually spans about an hour, allowing interviews to assess the thought process behind a large percentage of student work.

The child should be in charge of his own learning. By investigating one standard in a variety of ways, each child is able to find a medium that "talks" to him or her. Research suggests that girls might learn better cooperatively and that boys prefer competition. In Geoblock Match-Up, you might witness two girls working to fill a game board together; the boys may have competed and moved on! I step in at signs of little growth— someone who isn't acquiring the concept or who's failing to challenge himself. I tend to allow children with similar styles to work in groups. One child may verbalize or show an example, with my guidance. The other three may not have verbalized what was going on, but they will tend to copy this child's visual examples. Without probing these children to use their words to describe the process, visual modeling would probably succeed but leave communication vulnerable. My hope is that with the conclusion of this lesson, it seems we are well on our way to six-year-olds being fluent in *analyzing characteristics and properties of 2-D and 3-D geometric shapes and developing mathematical arguments about geometric relationships!* We'll learn even more as we help others replicate our success!

Reference

National Research Council. (2005). *How students learn: Mathematics in the classroom* (M. S. Donovan & J. D. Bransford, eds.). Washington, DC: National Academies Press.

⧉ 25. Using Writing to Teach Math

Ganna Maymind
Morganville, New Jersey

Recommended Level: Grades 1–5

Overall Objective: Students will demonstrate the ability to understand counting coins by writing in a math journal.

Materials Needed: A notebook for each student. This can be a composition book. I use a stenography notepad bought at the local office supply store.

To introduce counting coins read *Alexander, Who Used to Be Rich Last Sunday* by Judith Viorst (1978). Discuss with students what they already know about money and brainstorm a list of money words (*penny, quarter, dollar, change, bought, figured, counted, cost, store,* etc.). Type the word list and print as many copies as you have students, glue them on index cards, laminate them, and have students tape the word list to their desks.

The next day, pass out student math journals and review the word list you created. Tell students you have been thinking about counting coins and want to share a story. Write your story in front of the students, modeling your thinking as you go along. For example, I might write, "One summer day, I went for a walk on the boardwalk. I wanted to buy ice cream. It cost 1 dollar and 65 cents. I looked in my pocket. I had 1 dollar, 3 dimes, 2 nickels, and 2 pennies. I counted first by tens, 10, 20, 30, then by fives, 35, 40, and then by ones, 41, 42. I only had one dollar and 42 cents, which is less than 65, so I could not buy the ice cream." Ask students to think of a time they had to count coins to buy something, and have a couple of students share their story.

Before students write a story down, have them turn to the person sitting next to them and share their story. This gives them a chance to think out loud before they write. It also allows those students who don't know what to write about have someone help them come up with a story. Once students have shared with another student, they start writing. I encourage them to look at their math word list for help.

While the students are writing, walk around to conference with individual students and help them to write out their thinking. I also make sure to tell the students, "I will be reading all your math journals at the end of the day. But, I am not inside your head, so it is really important to show your thinking. Let the ideas flow from your brain, through your hand, and out through your pencil. I can't wait to read what you wrote!"

Once most students are finished writing their entries, they come on the rug and sit next to their writing partner. This is the same writing partner that the students have during writing workshop, so they are used to working with them. The partners are assigned a number, one or two, and I announce which partner will read their entry to the other partner first. The partner helps to peer edit the entry, as well as clarify everything to make sure it makes sense.

After students are done partner editing and revising, I pick two students to share their entries with the class. Most times, I select the two students ahead of time. The student that is sharing gets to wear a special hat (it is a plastic black hat with a yellow felt light bulb glued to the top). After sharing, the student asks for 2 questions or comments from the class. The student comments and questions range from, "I really liked your story," to "How did you come up with the idea?" Many times, sharing times are opportunities to teach the students something new. It is a chance for the curriculum to come from the students. For example, students have written about sales, tax being added on, and appropriate prices of things. This gives me a chance to further delve into these concepts rather than randomly teaching them to the students.

I have found that using math journals with any math concept can help even my low-performing students achieve more in math. Writing allows students to have those wonderful ideas and "Aha" moments that are so important in today's test-driven world. It is a chance for students to see the direct connection between learning and the real world. Isn't that the whole purpose?

Helpful Hints

Math journals can be used for any math concept, including time, fractions, and adding and subtracting. The examples given are for first grade. Math journals can also be used in Grades 2 through 5. The word list for each concept will be higher in complexity. Also, teacher modeling will align with what is expected from students. It might help to take well-written student entries and share them with the class using an overhead. This helps the students see what is expected. When assigning writing partners, I find it helpful to assign homogenous groups, so one student doesn't overpower the conversation.

Reference

Viorst, J. (1978). *Alexander, who used to be rich last Sunday.* New York: Atheneum.

26. Patterns With Toothpicks

Deb Guthrie
Arden Hills, Minnesota

Recommended Level: Grades 2–5

Objective: To practice using age-appropriate algebraic representations to describe polygons.

Standards Met (Minnesota):

Math: Understand patterns, relations, and functions; Represent and analyze mathematical situations and structures using algebraic symbols; Use mathematical models to represent and understand quantitative relationships; Analyze change in various contexts

Materials Needed:

- Toothpicks (about 50 per student)
- Paper and pencils (for making a t-chart and/or drawing pictures of the model)
- Centimeter-grid paper—one per student—for graphing

Activity:

1. Pass out supplies to the students. (I use 9×12 foam sheets to keep the toothpicks from sliding around.)

2. Using a document camera or overhead projector, demonstrate how to build the first stage of your model, using three toothpicks.

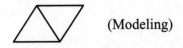   (Modeling)

3. Have them build the model at their desks. Then ask students to describe what they see. (Verbal description)

   One triangle

   Three toothpicks

   Equilateral triangle

4. Build on another triangle, so you have two triangles in a straight line.

   (Modeling)

5. Have students build on the additional triangle. Ask them to describe what they see. (Verbal description)

Two triangles

Parallelogram

Five toothpicks

6. Have a student come up to build the next triangle on the over-head or document camera.

   (Modeling)

7. Have students do it at their desks. Ask them, "What do you notice about this design?" (Verbal description)

Three triangles

Trapezoid

Thing elephants stand on in a circus

Seven toothpicks

Two "up" triangles, one "down" triangle

You want the triangles to continue in a straight line—not wrap around into a hexagon.

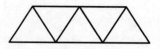

8. Ask the students, "How can we organize our information about the number of toothpicks we use in each design to help us predict the number of toothpicks for more triangles?" Hopefully, the students will have had experience with t-charts. If not, draw one on the board.

(Make table or chart)

Ask, "What does this look like?" (They will answer, "A T.") "Right. We call this a 't-chart.' This will help us organize our data so we can look for patterns. I'll label the first column 'Triangles.' What shall we label the second column?" (Wait for the children to say, "Toothpicks.") Have the children draw a t-chart on their paper. I don't give the children a worksheet with the t-chart already made. I think it benefits them to actually construct it themselves.

9. Ask, "What patterns do you see in the numbers on the t-chart?" (verbal description)

Triangles	Toothpicks
1	3
2	5
3	7

Number of triangles goes up by one

Number of toothpicks goes up by 2

10. Ask, "Who can come up and fill in the chart for five triangles?" and, "How did you know what to write?" The students can confirm the entries by building the triangles if necessary.

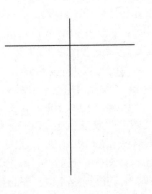

11. Ask, "Who can come up and fill in the chart for ten triangles?" (Have a vertical ellipses showing that you skipped some numbers on purpose in each column.) Ask the student, "How did you know what to write?" Ask the students how many toothpicks they would need for one hundred triangles. Ask, "How do you know?"

12. Hopefully, someone will notice that every new triangle takes two toothpicks. So the relationship between the number of triangles and the number of toothpicks is "number of triangles times two, plus one." Second graders may say, "Double the number of triangles and add one." When a student offers that relationship, say "How do you know?" Ask them, "Where does the 'times two' come from?" (Two toothpicks are used for every triangle we add on. Why only two? Because they are sharing a side with the previous triangle.) Ask, "Where does 'plus one' come from?" (Because you had to use three toothpicks on the first triangle, so it was two toothpicks *plus one*.) At this point, I would have them write the description of the pattern on their papers. (Verbal description)

13. Ask the students, "So, if I use n to represent 'any number,' how could we write a number model, or expression, for any number?" (The formula is $2n + 1$.)

14. If appropriate (and I have had second graders do this), graph the number of triangles on the horizontal axis and the number toothpicks on the vertical axis. I give the students grid paper, but I prefer that they label the axes, write the numbers on each axis, and write a title for the graph. Remind them to write the numbers right where the grid lines intersect the axes. Several of the students will probably make mistakes putting the numbers on the grid, so have some extra sheets available. It's a valuable experience for them. Again, if they always get prepared graphs, they won't think about how they are actually constructed. Students tend to have a great deal of experience with bar graphs and like to put the numbers in the middle of each space.

If you're going to extend this activity by doing the same thing with squares, have them draw little triangles at the coordinate points instead of dots. *Do not connect the points with a line, as you don't have fractions of triangles and fractions of toothpicks.* Just look at the shape the points make—it's a straight line. Then you can use the same graph to display the information for squares, pentagons, and so on. This activity can be extended to squares (3n + 1), pentagons (4n + 1), and so on. Make t-charts for each shape. All the data can be graphed on one graph, so you can see how the graph changes as the shapes have more toothpicks. The points for each shape will form straight lines.

Note: *Patterns With Toothpicks* was inspired by *The Math Solution: Teaching Mathematics Through Problem Solving,* by M. Burns, 1991, Sausalito, CA: Marilyn Burns Education Associates.

27. Math-A-Thon

Kelli Higgins
East Peoria, Illinois

Recommended Level: Grades 2–5

Overall Objective: To celebrate the beginning of our statewide standardized testing (ISAT—Illinois Standards Achievement Test) by reviewing math skills in a fun way.

Standards Met (Illinois):

Math: Develop fluency in adding, subtracting, multiplying, and dividing whole numbers; Understand the need for measuring with standard units and become familiar with standard units in the customary and metric systems; Carry out simple unit conversions, such as centimeters to meters, within a system of measurement; Develop understanding of fractions as parts of unit wholes, as parts of a collection, as locations on number lines, and as divisions of whole numbers; Use models, benchmarks, and equivalent forms to judge the size of fractions; Identify, compare, and analyze attributes of two- and three-dimensional shapes and develop vocabulary to describe the attributes; Build and draw geometric objects

Materials Needed:

- *The Doorbell Rang* by Pat Hutchins (1986)
- An assortment of cookies (one per child)
- *Twizzlers Shapes and Patterns* book by Jerry Pallotta (2002)
- Twizzlers Pull and Peel licorice (plan on two per child—one to use and one to eat)
- Liquid Measurement "Gallon Gal" poster or handouts
- *The Hershey's Milk Chocolate Bar Fractions Book* by Jerry Pallotta (1999)
- Hershey's chocolate bars (one full-size candy bar per child)
- 18" Paper craft straws (have hundreds on hand so you don't run out)
- Pipe cleaners (hundreds of them cut into four-inch sections)

Math-A-Thon Schedule

Reading: Share *The Doorbell Rang* by Pat Hutchins. Discuss how the whole story is a math problem. Demonstrate how to show division, as some kids have not learned it. Students will work on the math story problem worksheet. Each student will write for cookie story problems of their own using +, −, ×, and division.

When students complete their worksheets, they get to select and eat a cookie and complete a calculator fun worksheet as the rest of the class finishes.

Measurement Stations: Students will visit three stations to perform a stunt and measure the distance traveled. They will complete a standing long jump, a paper ball toss, and a heavy box shove. At each station, they will predict, perform, measure the distance, and record their results.

Twizzlers Pull and Peel Math: Share some of the book with the students. Review lines, angles, and circle information. Students will use Twizzlers to demonstrate understanding of each concept. When

The Doorbell Rang

By Pat Hutchins

1. The story does not tell how many cookies Ma baked. However, you are given some hints. She tells the two children to share them, and they say that they each get 6. Write a multiplication problem to show how many cookies Ma baked.

2. When two more friends come to the door, Ma tells the kids to share the cookies. You need to divide the total number of cookies by the total number of kids sharing. Write a division problem to show how many cookies each child gets now.

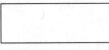

3. When the doorbell rings again, there are two more friends at the door. How many kids does that make? Write an addition problem to show the total number of kids.

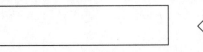

4. When the doorbell rings again, 6 more kids are at the door. That makes a total of 12 kids. How many cookies will each child get now?

5. When Grandma arrives, she brings more cookies. If each child now gets three cookies, how many cookies did Grandma bring? Show your work:

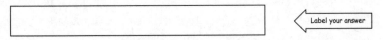

Before you can eat your cookie, you have to write four math questions of your own. Write one problem for addition, subtraction, multiplication, and division.

they have shown all of their work on their paper using licorice strips, they get it checked. They may eat the rest of their Twizzlers as they copy the work on their paper with pencil.

Liquid Measurement Comparisons: Share "Gallon Gal," as a visual demonstration of liquid measurement, and fill in the blanks with the students. Students will use the "Gallon Gal" visual to make comparisons and complete a worksheet.

Hershey Fraction Math: Share some of the book with students. Discuss fractions as part of a whole. The whole is the total number of parts that you are starting with. Talk about the numerator and the denominator. Show samples on the board. Students use their Hershey bar to complete the worksheet. When they are done, they can eat their candy.

3-D Figure Construction: Demonstrate how to create 3-D shapes using paper straws and pipe cleaners. Students must measure their pieces with a ruler, and they must cut the straws with scissors. They will cut and bend pipe cleaners so they are doubled over to connect the pieces of their figure together. Students can complete more than one if time allows.

Pentominoes Station: Have multiple sets of pentominoes and puzzle cards on hand. As faster students finish each of the planned activities, they need anchor activities to keep them engaged in mathematics.

References

Hutchins, P. (1986). *The doorbell rang.* New York: Greenwillow Books.
Pallotta, J. (1999). *The Hershey's Milk Chocolate Bar fractions book.* Needham, MA: Corporate Board Books.
Pallotta, J. (2002). *Twizzlers shapes and patterns.* New York: Scholastic.

Gallon Gal

Label each part of Gallon Gal with gallon, quarts, pints, and cups.

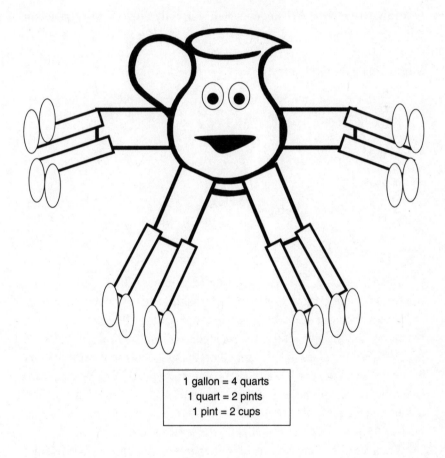

1 gallon = 4 quarts
1 quart = 2 pints
1 pint = 2 cups

▧ 28. Problem Solving

Debbie Gordon
Phoenix, Arizona

Recommended Level: Grades 3–5

Overall Objective: All students will correctly solve a story problem with 85% accuracy.

Standards Met (Arizona):

Number sense and operations: Solve word problems using grade-level appropriate operations

Materials:

- Pencil
- Copy of story problem

Opening Set

Read *Stacks of Trouble* by Martha F. Brenner (2000)—a story that uses multiplication and addition for washing dishes, but any similar story may be used—to the class but not telling the answers to the problems within the story. The teacher will select one of the dish problems for the class to solve together, then students will work in pairs to solve several other math problems embedded within the story (whiteboards and markers will be available if needed). This lesson differentiates multiplication problem solving to meet the individual needs of the students in a typical math classroom.

Each year, my classroom of students is made up of a wide range of mathematical levels and abilities. As an elementary teacher with an ever-increasing number of boys and girls, I have struggled with trying to find a way to meet their diverse needs within my daily math lessons. I have found using story problems is very effective to this end, and they are an efficient tool for my own planning and assessment. Story problems are an excellent way to practice and reinforce computation skills as well as critical-thinking skills. The story problem in the lesson practices basic multiplication skills embedded within a realistic context. I purposefully chose the numbers in the problem so that every one of my students *could* solve the problem. The numbers in my story problems usually vary from below grade level to above grade level, thus allowing for that wide span of learners I have in my room.

When I write story problems, I write one problem for the entire class and instead of filling in the spot where the number would have gone, I leave it blank, and at the bottom of the problem, I provide several different numbers. My thinking is to allow my students to choose the appropriate number for them to insert into the problem.

My students are thrilled with the opportunity to make their own choices about their learning, and it shows in the interest, enthusiasm, accuracy, and confidence with which they solve the problems. We talk quite a bit about choosing the right number to use, and the students learn very quickly that the right choice will make a difference in their ability to solve a problem correctly.

I have found that, by providing students with a full range of numbers to use when solving story problems, I can watch my struggling students gain the confidence and success they desperately need to improve their understanding and growth in mathematics. I also see my higher learners continue to learn, grow, and be challenged in a regular math class. And, I have cut my planning time in half while writing story problems for my students to solve. I now only need one set of math problems, and I can easily adjust the numbers to meet the various needs of all the diverse learners in my classroom.

Guiding Questions

Can you help Mike figure out how many dishes he had to wash?

Check for Understanding and Accuracy

How did you figure out how many bowls there were? (2 groups of 8 or 4 + 4 = 8)

How many plates were on the shelf? (12)

Did anyone solve this problem another way?

Independent Practice

Students will solve the pencil story problem below.

If pencils cost 9¢ each, and Mrs. Gordon bought _____ pencils, how much money did she spend?

(4)   (15)   (24)   (8)

Accommodations for Individual Needs

Students will have a choice of numbers to use so that each student can solve the problem according to their individual skill level and understanding of the mathematical operations. Struggling students generally choose the smaller numbers whereas the higher-level thinkers choose the larger numbers. The teacher will be available for additional help and support as needed, and will monitor students' work while walking about the room.

The teacher will bring the students together to share solutions to the problem. Students will first share their thinking with the person next to them. Then the teacher will ask several students to write their solution strategies on the front board and explain their strategies. The teacher will collect the problems and check them for accuracy.

Reference

Brenner, M. F. (2000). *Stacks of trouble.* New York: Kane Press.

🖻 29. Exploring Side Lengths of Triangles and Quadrilaterals

Pam Cyr
Shelburne, Vermont

Recommended Level: Grade 5

Overall Objective: To understand and use the language of geometry to communicate mathematical ideas; to build and classify triangles and quadrilaterals; to discover that the sum of any two side lengths of a triangle is greater than the length of the third side; to discover that the sum of any three side lengths of a quadrilateral is greater than the length of the fourth side.

Standards Met (NCTM):

Math: Use the language of mathematics to express mathematical ideas precisely; Analyze characteristics and properties of two-dimensional geometric shapes and develop mathematical arguments about geometric relationships; Identify, compare, and analyze attributes of two-dimensional shapes and develop vocabulary to describe the attributes; Classify two-dimensional shapes according to their properties and develop definitions of classes of shape; Explore congruence and similarity; Make and test conjectures about geometric properties and relationships and develop logical arguments to justify conclusions; Use visualization, spatial reasoning, and geometric modeling to solve problems; Build and draw geometric objects

Materials Needed:

- Shapes sets
- Pencils
- Graphic organizers
- Math dictionaries
- Polystrips

- Brass fasteners
- Chart paper
- Markers
- Triangle Blackline sheet
- Problem-solving question

Every mathematics program I have encountered has had crucial components missing from units and lessons. These prescribed programs need to be reviewed with a critical eye. As informed educators, we need to preview the goals and objectives and ask, "What do my students need to be successful?" More often than not, the language of mathematics is a barrier to that success. Another missing feature I find is *nonexamples*. Over and over, examples are provided. However, students also need to see nonexamples to fully grasp concepts. I also find that lessons assume students will construct rules and make generalizations with only limited exposure to the mathematical idea at hand.

The lessons described below have been adapted from the Connected Math Programs' *Shapes and Design* unit (Lappan, Fey, Fitzgerald, Friel, & Philips, 2006). In previewing this unit, it was obvious to me that a vocabulary component needed to be included. I also predicted that students would not be able to construct the triangle inequality rule with the limited experience provided in the text. I revamped the lessons to include both.

Preteaching

I begin the unit by asking the students, "What is a polygon?" This leads to a discussion of prefixes such as *tri, quad, hex, hept,* and *oct.* We agree that a polygon is *a closed shape made of line segments with many sides.* We then use this definition for other polygons, replacing "many" with the specific number named by the prefix.

Classifying Triangles

I hand out triangle shape sets to each table group and ask the children, "How can you sort these triangles?" We discuss how and why the triangles are classified. The terms *equilateral, scalene, right,* and *isosceles* flow into our conversation. Together, we complete a graphic organizer. The class agrees upon a definition for *triangle* and refers to math dictionaries for verification. Students sketch examples and non-examples of triangles and label these appropriately using previously discussed terms that define types of triangles.

Building Triangles

Once children have sorted, discussed properties of, and sketched different types of triangles, I hand out polystrips. These manipulatives are plastic strips that can be pieced together with brass fasteners to form polygons. Ten minutes is given to free exploration, and we talk about using this manipulative as a tool, rather than a toy. I model how to count the side lengths, counting spaces between two holes as one unit. We observe the fact that triangles have to be stable figures and not collapse. I make a large chart and write *Equilateral, Scalene, Right,* and *Isosceles* in columns on the board. I ask students, "What three side lengths form these different types of triangles?" Students use the polystrips to build at least one of each type of triangle, and then they record the side lengths under the correct category. With skillful guidance, a discussion about *congruency* and *similarity* occurs as side lengths are recorded. Children recognize congruency by comparing triangles with their peers. As they flip and turn these polygons, they realize they are exactly the same. Similarity is easy to visualize with equilateral triangles. Children understand that even though the length of the side lengths grow larger, proportion remains constant.

Building Nontriangles

Next, I add a column to our chart, *Side Lengths That Don't Work.* I ask children, "What three side lengths won't form a triangle?" Students use three polystrips and find side lengths that won't connect to form a triangle. I model an example, and the children eagerly get started with their exploration. Again, these side lengths are recorded. After each child has recorded at least two examples, we stop and observe our findings. I ask the children, "What patterns do you notice on the chart? How could we know which side lengths will join together to form a triangle without having to build it?" Students talk in small groups and then report their observations to the larger group. If most of the children construct the idea that the sum of any given side lengths has to be greater than the third side length to form a triangle, we record the rule and refer to our chart of side lengths to prove it works. More often than not, though, kids have difficulty extrapolating this rule.

Discovering the Triangle Inequality Theorem

I ask the children to build and sketch triangles with side lengths 4,4,8; 4,4,9; 4,4,7; 4,4,3; 3,5,8; 3,5,9; 3,5,7; and 3,5,4. I ask them, "How could we figure out which side lengths will join together to form a triangle without having to build it?" Through this hands-on investigation, students notice that the figures with side lengths 4,4,8 and 3,5,8 collapse. They observe that triangles can be only be constructed with side lengths 4,4,7; 4,4,3; 3,5,7; and 3,5,4. By keeping the first two side lengths constant, the children focus their attention on what's different about the third side length. Most students, at this point, construct the rule that the sum of any two side lengths of a triangle must be greater than the third side length to form a triangle. After elated whoops of discovery have filled the room, we go back to our original chart and prove our rule works. The children's egos are inflated with success!

Extending Knowledge With Quadrilaterals

Vocabulary

I hand out quadrilateral shape sets to the students and ask, "How can these quadrangles be sorted?" Working in small groups, students sort the quadrilaterals. Classifications are discussed and agreed upon. Conversations are filled with terms such as *quadrangles, rhombus, trapezoid, parallelogram, square,* and *rectangle.* After groups share how they sorted the shapes, I hand out a vocabulary graphic organizer with the focus on *quadrilateral.* We complete it with a rich discussion of a definition, examples, and nonexamples of quadrilaterals. Sketches are constructed and labeled.

Building Quadrilaterals and Nonquadrilaterals

I make a large chart on the board with columns labeled *Trapezoid, Parallelogram,* and *Other Quadrilaterals.* I ask students, "Which four side lengths will form different types of quadrilaterals?" Students build quadrangles and record side lengths. Again, the concepts of *similarity* and *congruence* are discussed as children explore. After everyone has had the opportunity to build and record a couple of different quadrangles, I add another column to our chart and label it *Non-quadrilateral.* I ask, "Which four side lengths will not form a quadrangle?" After children investigate and record findings, we stop and have a group discussion. I ask, "What patterns do you notice? How can you tell if four side lengths will form a quadrilateral without building it?" Prior experience with triangles allows most children to easily construct the rule that the sum of any three side lengths must be greater than the fourth side length to form a quadrilateral.

I then pose the question, "How many different quadrilaterals can be constructed with a set of given side lengths?" The children busily build and sketch quadrangles. *Congruency* is discussed again and again. Through trial and error, students learn that three different quadrilaterals can be formed with a set of given side lengths.

Extending Knowledge

The question is raised, "What can we generalize about building any polygon with a given number of side lengths?" Students make conjectures. We list these conjectures on the board, then children work in small groups to test them out. Children are able to connect what they have learned about triangle and quadrilateral side lengths to other polygons' side lengths.

Enduring Knowledge

A couple of months after this investigation, I give students a problem to solve to assess enduring knowledge of previously explored concepts. The majority of my students are able to successfully solve this problem by using diagrams and generalizing a rule. They can do this because they constructed their knowledge! Children self-assess their solutions by using our problem-solving rubric, and it is kept as evidence of learning in each student's math portfolio. At conference time, children share this documentation with parents along with his or her story of learning through hands-on exploration.

I taught this series of related lessons over the course of a week. As you can probably tell, I thoroughly enjoy tearing apart prescribed units and making them my own. Reworking lessons to meet my students' needs is a necessity, not a luxury. My effort and time are more than rewarded when I experience successful learners who use the language of mathematics, make conjectures, test theories, and learn from great mistakes.

Reference

Lappan, G., Fey, J. T., Fitzgerald, W. M., Friel, S. N., & Philips, E. (2006). *Connected mathematics 2: Shapes and designs: Two-dimensional geometry.* Boston: Pearson, Prentice Hall, 2006.

30. Fundraiser Math

Shari Kaneshiro
Honolulu, Hawaii

Recommended Level: Grade 5

Overall Objective: Fifth-grade students use their critical-thinking, problem-solving, and mathematical skills to help with their school's annual fundraiser.

Standards Met (Hawaii):

Geometry: Use visualization, special reasoning, and geometric modeling to solve problems

Measurement: Understand measurable attributes of objects and the units, systems, and processes of measurement; Apply appropriate techniques, tools, and formulas to determine measurements

Problem Solving: Apply and adapt a variety of appropriate strategies to solve problems

Service Learning

Materials Needed:

- Plastic cones
- Field lining string
- Field lining paint
- Meter tape
- Calculators
- Paper
- Pencils

Each year, our school holds an annual fundraiser. We call it a "Fun Run." The Fun Run involves all students, from kindergarten through Grade 5, gathering pledges for each lap that they run in 30 minutes. In order to keep it safe, the circular track is divided into two tracks. The inside track would be used by kindergarten through second-grade students, and the larger, outer track for third- through fifth-grade students. Our oldest students (fifth grade) take pride in running the most laps. Students look forward to this event as they raise money for their school and challenge themselves in endurance and speed.

One particular year, the students were disappointed in their number of total laps at the end of the Fun Run. As we held a discussion, many students felt that their track was much larger than the previous year. Other students were wondering how this would affect the fundraising effort since the number of laps was less than other years.

Since my school is very involved in service learning, I decided to use the Fun Run and integrate it into my teaching.

I told my class that we would be the design center for this year's Fun Run. They would work in teams and design a track for the Fun Run, keeping in mind the time frame for the event, the students involved, and the fact that it is a fundraiser. Students were given access to the fifth-grade data of laps run from the previous year.

The assignment for each team was to (1) design a running track for kindergarten through second grade and a track for third through fifth grade, (2) show how they used circumference and area for a circle in their design, (3) display knowledge of converting from one unit of measurement to another, (4) draw out their design on graph paper, providing a scale, and (5) explain in detail their design. And they had to answer the question, "Why should the class vote for your group's model as the winner?"

The students became involved in this project right away. Each group worked on their proposals, calculating and comparing data from the previous year's Fun Run.

Determining the track length was a question that posed problems for many students. They found that if they made the track too short, students could run too many laps and parents might not be able to afford their pledge per-lap amount. They also found that if they made the track too long, students may not run as many laps, and the fundraising would not be as successful.

We also took our math class outside to the field so that they could use their measuring tools and visualize their creations on the actual field.

Once all the groups were done with their design and written explanations, each group presented their proposal to the entire class. A
question/answer session was held after each presentation.

The second part of the project involved the students all taking part
in actually lining the track on the field according to the configurations
of the winning design. It is in this section that the students would use
the meter tape, paint, cones, and string.

Upon completing the project, the students were so proud of their
accomplishments in this grand activity. In fact, I think that because they
were involved in the project from beginning to end, the students felt
ownership and took the Fun Run more seriously than in previous years.
Since the fifth grade has been involved in designing the track for our
Fun Run, we have always surpassed our goal for fundraising.

PART **III**

Teaching Reading and Writing

Teaching Reading

Overview, Chapters 31–35

31. **Peggy J. Billiard**, an elementary school librarian from Logansport, Indiana, brought a reading program to her school that dramatically increased independent reading among students Grades K–5. By introducing them to ability-appropriate literature, Peggy fostered a love for independent reading in her school.

32. **Jodi Jari,** an English as a second language teacher in Oshkosh, Wisconsin, teaches students English through movement of the body. Her students acquire English vocabulary in the same way they learned their native language—through demonstration and modeling.

33. **Maranda Alcalá,** an English language development specialist in Fairview, Oregon, introduces students to nonfiction books using *More Trees, Please!* In this weeklong lesson, the students learn about trees, about the elements in a nonfiction book, and even get to create a flip-flap book themselves.

34. **Reid Nunn**, a fourth- and fifth-grade multiage classroom teacher from Albuquerque, uses a reading assessment menu to let students explore their different intelligences. Students get to interview a classmate, act out a skit, or draw a comic strip to illustrate what they've learned about their reading.

35. **Karen Ann Brown**, a fourth-grade gifted teacher in Littleton, Colorado, gets students excited about research on a topic of their choice. Karen introduces her students to research papers and the elements of nonfiction. The students create an electronic book to present their findings to the class.

31. The Elementary Teacher-Librarian

A Job Defined by the Needs of the School

Peggy J. Billiard
Logansport, Indiana

Recommended Level: Grades K–5

Overall Objective: To create a reading program and increase reading levels in elementary schools. Students will gain a love for reading through reading age- and reading-level-appropriate material.

Throughout my first twenty-eight years in education, the elementary library changed from a separate room for storing books to a planned library in a new building with consolidation. The position of elementary librarian was created in our district. The school with low test scores had a high turnover in the position, and the job was posted again. No one with a library science degree had applied, but I had acquired a master's degree in reading education.

I imagined what the elementary school library would be if it were a storage room for just my classroom! Using my teaching experiences from grades 1, 2, 4, and 5 as a foundation, I began organizing for the school's needs with the increasing accountability. A total school reading program would positively impact student test scores and simultaneously justify retaining a library teaching position in a windfall of budget cuts. My plan included promoting reading, teaching standards-based minilessons to support classroom instruction, and managing materials for the needs of students and teachers.

The love of reading would help students become life-long learners and increase test scores. I gathered real data: Only about 33% of the students in the school earned ten or more reader points in the independent reading program. Our students were not adequately participating, and older students read easy books markedly under their reading levels. I monitored the reading climate of both teachers and students and helped create a pleasant, enthusiastic atmosphere, which valued and encouraged reading, connecting the library and classrooms. Students with a wide variety of interests entered the library looking for a good book to read for pleasure or information. As the teacher-librarian, I helped students by talking with them individually to find out what they needed and liked in books (Brassell, 2006). The school library needed to provide quality literature with rich language through many types of great stories and different genres and titles. Writing grants helped subsidize a slim budget.

When children read books they *could* read, at the right difficulty and age level, they gradually moved smoothly to higher reading levels (Church, 2003). As the teacher-librarian, I could monitor the types of materials chosen, by both topic and level, to match students with books so they could increase their reading levels and skills. High-interest books with photographs were used to entice all students into books. Reluctant readers needed more encouragement and books they liked (Bishop, 2003). High-ability students needed quality literature . . . and lots of it. Students also needed help choosing progressively harder types of books: Picture books, easy readers, and short chapter books, all of which precede the longer chapter books students usually read in middle school. Students soon learned to self-select more appropriate books.

Using a coding system of leveling (below third grade and at half-grade increments) on the spines of books helped students more easily select books at their levels (Morrow, 2002). To double-check each student's book choices, his or her independent reading level was recorded on the back of the individual library checkout card. Some students wanted to check out books for an adult to read with or to them. While helping students choose books, I continued to invite them to try many different types of books.

Through an electronic reading system, using Accelerated Reader, I teamed with classroom teachers in motivating and managing students' independent reading. I attended training and provided professional development for teachers in our building. Through such a system, students read books, take a computer test, and keep track of their individual points. A daily record log of reading helped students begin longer chapter books. Teachers became more aware of reports from the program to assist in their communication with parents and grade-level team data collection. These reports also helped identify reading problems in comprehension and vocabulary.

The entire school was determined to increase the amount of time students spent reading. By providing time for independent reading, students began to develop a solid foundation for literacy development and a habit of reading for enjoyment. According to Thompson (1991), "Research has shown that the more opportunities children have to read independently, the better readers they will become" (p. 14). A regular routine time for students' reading was established in classrooms and the library. With clear expectations for students and monitoring of their book selections, all staff supported student success. What began as individual goal sheets for students during library time resulted in many students earning 10 new points each grading term. Total school reading points nearly doubled from the previous year, at 8,000, to over 15,000 points. This practice from the library program was changed into a requirement by the schoolwide planning team, requiring every student in Grades 2 through 5 to earn 15 new points during each grading period. Students were encouraged to continuously read instead of just attaining a point level. The more time students read, the better their reading skills developed, and test scores started to climb.

A motivation plan with small rewards involving the entire school helped students reach their individual goals and do their individual best. Students received prizes for their achievement during library classes. In the beginning, prize levels were more frequent, but now have been changed to the following: 10 points (bookmark, ruler, or pen), 20 points (reader pin, pencil eraser, or folder), 35 points (reading racer bracelet received during the morning closed-circuit announcements), 60 points (backpack or pencil case with four or five small items), and 100 points and each successive 50 points (prize from a shelf of book fair items chosen by students). Point levels and prizes are changed yearly with student and teacher input. All prizes are purchased with monies from ink cartridge recycling and book fair profits or bonuses. Certificates are presented to students, by their teachers, during each grading period awards ceremony. When students were taught to set clear goals, they began to plan to meet the goals and succeed. Students not only became readers but they learned life skill planning. By informing parents, support and encouragement could be established at home (Brassell, 2006).

Special activities in the library helped students learn to love the library and reading. Schoolwide book fairs, special author days, and writing projects encouraged students to get even more involved with books. Creating more of a bookstore atmosphere in the library promoted sharing books (Brassell, 2006), and students talked about visiting bookstores and libraries outside of school.

As the teacher-librarian with wide experiences as a reading teacher, I could offer a variety of literacy experiences for students, such as modeling reading behaviors and teaching minilessons to increase students' reading skills. Reading aloud to children always helps them comprehend the plot of the story and leads to better independent reading. Book talks promoted reading in different types of books and were used to connect the library to content areas in the classroom (Church, 2003). Students began to encourage each other and share books they liked (Brassell, 2006) through book discussions and talks in small groups. Special programs, such as a question competition with books or special areas for stories written by staff and students, encouraged the entire school to be more involved with books. Displays of books on certain topics or by special authors enticed students. Lists of good books to read aloud and other special booklists were shared with classroom teachers to promote independent reading and special reading in the classroom (Pitcher & Mackey, 2004).

As a staff member, I was already trained in the foundation of teaching and could provide quality lesson plans with teaching techniques for all learners (Shannon, 2006). A strong literacy program with an instructional supportive role in collaboration with teachers seemed critical (Kaplan, 2007). Because teachers are required to do more and more, the library program could support both teachers and students in the entire school. The gradual development of partnerships with classroom teachers began to result in support for collaboratively planned units with shared teaching, planning, and resources (Kaplan, 2007). Intentional communication with busy classroom teachers encouraged them to ask for information and materials for units and lessons.

The school library became more of an extension of the regular classrooms. When the school library program became more integrated into the curriculum with minilessons, students began to reap the benefits with higher achievement (Shannon, 2006). Students have a wide variety of needs and many ranges of reading levels. As the teacher-librarian I continued to be aware of individual student needs, know the texts available, as well as understand the reading process (Fountas & Pinnell, 1999). Students benefited from lessons on information skills and comprehension skills including recognizing the author, purpose, main idea, plot, setting, and characterization of a text, and they developed inference skills and vocabulary (Bishop, 2003). Younger students and students acquiring a new language benefited from lessons incorporating concepts about print, language acquisition, and vocabulary knowledge (Brassell, 2006). By using guided reading lesson components, I used shared reading to expand vocabulary, increase fluency, and reinforce sight words (Allen, 2002). Students then used library books one to two levels below the instructional level to practice the skills learned (Fountas & Pinnell, 1999). Library lessons complemented and provided additional minilessons on the language arts standards and allowed students to apply learning independently as well as offer follow-up activities for teachers.

As the teacher-librarian, I continually foster independence in using library materials to support standards in the schoolwide curriculum (Shannon, 2006). More than ever, students today need to have skills that will teach competency in finding, evaluating, and using viable information (Turner, 1985). Taught in conjunction with and integrated into both library lesson plans, I started teaching information skills to support increased student achievement. Our next step will be to agree upon a district-adopted research model for kindergarten through fifth grade, taught through all library programs, to help students continually learn to use information and apply the skills (Church, 2003). Students may need guidance in becoming effective users of information and ideas in many formats, from books to the Internet (Kaplan, 2007). Materials in the library should include all kinds of media to teach students how and when to use them. Books can be used for in-depth study and higher-level thinking skills, while Web sites are more appropriate for factual information. Students need to evaluate whether such sites are biased or incomplete (Aronson, 2007). Poetry, drama, and even picture books can be used to teach information skills (Miller, 2001).

Teacher-librarians must commit to a position of leadership by serving on the schoolwide planning team for curriculum, instruction, and partnership with the corporation technology team (Shannon, 2006). The philosophy, goals, and objectives of the total school must be supported with input and planning from the teacher-librarian in developing the library program. A needs assessment and a survey of how school programs were being used helped the staff focus on the strengths and weaknesses of the school, both of which can be supported through the library program.

Several research studies in numerous states show a strong library program can positively impact achievement test scores of students. Locally, the teacher-librarian must collect and organize data from the entire school and share the information with the schoolwide planning team and administration. The teacher-librarian must know the school, know the programs and materials, and commit to supporting improvements to positively impact learning (Turner, 1985) and collaborate with teachers and be involved in curriculum and instruction. Brassell (2006) summarizes current research and strongly suggests that teacher-librarians keep informed to make instruction and library practices effective. Church's (2003) chronological summary of library research from 1993 to 2002 highlighted the Colorado study that showed fourth graders increased as much as 18% on achievement tests because of library services. A strong library program designed for the school can overcome obstacles such as low socioeconomic or ethnic demographics (Church, 2003).

Our school critically needed a literacy library with a leveled book collection with a balance of fiction and nonfiction available for teachers to use with instructional groups. I began this collection with several boxes of paperbacks I previously used in my classroom and expanded with each book fair and with grant monies (Fountas & Pinnell, 1999). There is neither enough room in classrooms nor available finances to provide teachers with materials for small instructional groups. These paperback sets of books, organized alphabetically for each guided reading level, and stored in a section away from the student collection, made the library a literacy center for the needs of staff and students (Pitcher & Mackey, 2004). With in-house staff development for teaching guided reading, teachers began using leveled materials with small groups, and students steadily progressed to higher reading levels.

Materials selection and collection management help support and align the library with curriculum standards. Reminding teachers and students what materials are available to meet standards will increase use of the materials. All types of materials can coexist in the library and be made available to teachers and students. I worked to weed out old books and purchase appropriate new books in the management of the size and quality of the collection to positively impact student achievement by aligning more closely to state standards. Collection development, organization of materials, and management of the school library are essential to a strong library program. A wide variety of materials will give a diverse student population choice of genre and topics to help them become confident readers. For students whose first language is Spanish, I purchased Spanish books. When new materials arrived, I displayed them on a special shelf for viewing by students and teachers (Turner, 1985).

Besides teachers participating in selecting materials for instructional units, students should have input in selecting materials of interest or unit of study. Age-appropriate books of good quality were key to a strong collection (Kaplan, 2007). I utilized a school library book company to analyze the school library collection in terms of quantity and quality, including publication dates and circulation data (Kearney, 2000). All data should be considered with state standards and curriculum in mind, so outdated materials can be replaced (Church, 2003). I realize it will take a few years and a lot of money to attain a complete, balanced, and updated blue ribbon collection, but there were specific areas in the nonfiction collection that needed immediate attention. The dinosaur books were falling apart!

I established a working relationship with public librarians to network and provide better services to students (Bishop, 2003). The public library nonfiction collection provides a wider variety of topics and essentially extends the elementary library collection. Public library events and partnership events are advertised in the elementary school to encourage students to regularly visit the public library. One summer, I worked at the public library as a Parent Literacy Coach, helping and encouraging parents and children as they arrived to choose books. If students read books from the public library during the summer months, they are less likely to regress in their reading levels. Encouraging students to read outside of school can result in positive reading achievement and general school success.

In summary, the elementary teacher-librarian is a key staff member. Promoting reading, teaching lessons to support achievement, and managing the collection of materials can positively effect student achievement. As the teacher-librarian supports the entire staff, the administration and schoolwide planning team form a partnership with the teacher-librarian to develop a program for the needs of the school.

Are we finished with everything on our list? No. Have we made great gains during the past seven years? Yes. Was the elementary library a key to the improvements? Yes. Grade levels one through five are approaching 100% of the students earning 10 independent reader points, compared to our beginning of 33%. The first year, we awarded 100-point trophies to eight students. As we approach the end of the school year, about fifty students will receive a trophy for 100 points. The school language arts scores continue to climb with these and other continued efforts.

References

Allen, M. (2002). *Balancing literacy: A balanced approach to reading and writing instruction.* Huntington Beach, CA: Creative Teaching Press.

Aronson, M. (2007). Do books still matter? *School Library Journal. 53,* 36–39.

Bishop, K. (2003). *Connecting libraries with classrooms: The curricular roles of the media specialist.* Worthington, OH: Linworth.

Brassell, D. (2006). *Readers for life: The ultimate reading fitness guide, K–8.* Portsmouth, NH: Heinemann.

Church, A. P. (2003). *Leverage your library program to help raise test scores: A guide for library media specialists, principals, teachers, and parents.* Worthington, OH: Linworth.

Fountas, I. C., & Pinnell, G. S. (1999). *Matching books to readers: Using leveled books in guided reading, K–3.* Portsmouth, NH: Heinemann.

Kaplan, A. G. (2007). Is your school librarian "highly qualified"? *Phi Delta Kappan, 49,* 300–03.

Kearney, C. A. (2000). *Curriculum partner: Redefining the role of the library media specialist.* Westport, CT: Greenwood Press.

Laycock, K. (2003). School libraries and student achievement. *Teacher Librarian, 31,* 34.

Miller, P. (2001). *Reaching every reader: Promotional strategies for the elementary school library media specialist.* Worthington, OH: Linworth.

Morrow, L. M. (2002). *Literacy center: Contexts for reading and writing.* Portland, Maine: Stenhouse.

Pitcher, S. M., & Mackey, B. (2004). *Collaborating for real literacy: Librarian, teacher, and principal.* Worthington, OH: Linworth.

Shannon, D. (2006, September 27). Education and competencies of school library media specialists. *School Library Media Research.* Retrieved April 08, 2009, from http://www.ala.org/ala/aasl/aasl pubsandjournals/slmrb/slmrcontents/volume52002/shannon.cfm

Thompson, G. (1991). *Choosing and using trade books in the classroom.* New York: Scholastic.

Turner, P. (1985). *A school library media specialist's role: Helping teachers teach.* Littleton, CO: Libraries Unlimited.

32. Total Physical Response (TPR)

Learning Vocabulary Through Movement

Jodi Jari
Oshkosh, Wisconsin

Recommended Level: Grades 1–5 or new English as a second language students

Overall Objective: This second language acquisition program will help English language learners improve their vocabulary.

The premise of TPR is the understanding of English through the movement of the body. It is a natural way to learn, plus students retain more information when movement is involved. TPR was developed as a teaching strategy for the following reasons:

- It allows students to acquire vocabulary in a manner based on how a child learns a first language.
- Language input is comprehensible, which allows students to learn language naturally.

- The technique is hands-on, so students are involved to a greater extent.
- TPR is very direct and visual. This helps students learn vocabulary quicker and retain it longer.

TPR is a valuable tool when teaching ESL students; however, *all* children can use this technique with great success! TPR promotes active listening skills, increases comprehension, and develops vocabulary. I have also found the use of TPR helps students feel less stress, thus a feeling of trust can be established early on.

In the early stages of learning, this technique allows a student to observe actions. No oral response in English is necessary. Students can be in a silent period of language acquisition and yet be actively learning the English language. The basis of TPR is

- A series of commands that helps develop listening skills in the target language;
- Understanding developed through body movement;
- Target-language speech produced after exposure and practice; and
- Students listening to a command and following the action demonstrated.

Example of a Very Basic Lesson:

The teacher models and naturally says, "Stand up," and stands up while motioning students to do the same. Next, the teacher models and says, "Sit down," and sits down while motioning students to sit. This sequence of commands is repeated several times until students can demonstrate the action with confidence.

Students learning English need information delivered at their level. Language and content complexity can be increased after background knowledge has been established. TPR, as a method, lends itself beautifully to scaffolding the development of language skills. I have used this technique in one-on-one situations, with small groups, and with the class as a whole. Gestures, manipulatives, and pictures used along with TPR activities only enhance effectiveness.

Scaffolding Sequence

Skill Level	Activity	Literacy Level
Very easy	"This is a star. Point to the star."	Listening
	"Go to the door." "Touch the board."	Doing
	"Pick up the square, and give it to Sally."	
	"Draw a circle on the paper."	Drawing
	"Draw a circle on the bottom of the paper."	
	Describe a diagram for students to draw.	
	Partner practice—describe diagrams to each other.	Speaking
	Student leads whole class in activity.	
	Write commands on cards— students read cards.	Reading
Advanced	Students write commands for others to follow.	Writing

The strategy of TPR can be easily incorporated into content-area lesson plans to strengthen vocabulary and concept comprehension. Often, units of instruction in science or social studies involve specialized vocabulary that students may never have encountered previously. A quick base needs to be built in order to make further connections and so students learning English are able to participate to some degree from the onset.

TPR is a great way to learn what a student knows. Paper and pencil assessments may be beyond the student's ability level in English. These assessments do not always give a clear picture of the student's ability because of the language interference. Students can demonstrate processes, vocabulary, and sequences through the use of TPR.

The following is an example of TPR lessons for the subject areas of language and social studies. I have included them so that teachers can see how simple it is to integrate this strategy into their current units of study. I also included a TPR template for teachers to use as a simple outline for developing their own TPR lessons quickly and easily.

TPR Lesson

Subject: Social Studies—Safety Signs

1. Identify the vocabulary for the unit.

Stop sign	Hospital	Poison
School	Don't walk	Bathroom
Traffic light	Exit	Railroad
Walk	Go slow	Street sign

2. Ask yourself: Can any of these be acted out? Pantomimed? Are flashcards needed? Do I have any actual pictures?

3. Introduce the vocabulary words.

   a. Read a book or take a walk, and point out signs around the school. Point to the signs, and say, "Signs." Students could also draw the signs they see.
   b. Show and talk about a few chosen signs.

   For example: For a Hospital sign, identify the color, shape, and letters, and introduce the vocabulary words *doctor* and *sick.*

   For a School sign, identify the color, shape, and picture, and give the word *walking.*

   Students will respond at their level. Some will listen, others will repeat the key information, while still others will answer basic questions.

   c. Repeat the name of the signs several times while pointing to them.

   d. Hang up signs for easy student access. Add commands for the students to follow: "Point to the Exit sign." "Touch the sign that means *walk*."

   e. Repeat steps b through d daily, for a few minutes, while adding more signs.

Adaptations

- Partner students to practice vocabulary flashcards. Native speakers are excellent role models for second language learners.
- Make a book with the signs and key information.
- Draw the sign by listening to a description.

TPR Lesson Template

Subject

1. Identify the vocabulary for the unit.

2. Ask yourself: Can any of these be acted out? Pantomimed? Are flashcards needed? Do I have any actual pictures?

3. Introduce vocabulary words.

   a. Read a book, use real objects, show pictures, draw representations, or pantomime key content-area ideas.

   b. Demonstrate and discuss word meaning for a few chosen vocabulary words. Allow students to respond at their level.

   c. Repeat the words several times while pointing to objects or pictures, or while acting them out.

   d. Add commands for students to follow.

   e. Repeat steps b through d daily, for a few minutes, while adding more words each day.

HelpfulTips

- I find that TPR is great for parent helpers or peers to use. The method is easy and does not require a lot of direction or instructions from the teacher. A basic explanation is all that is needed. Success will follow!
- Overuse of TPR can lead to boredom. You do not want to use this tool for all lessons.
- Teachers must be flexible when planning their lessons. Changes may need to occur instantly depending on students' needs.
- When teaching abstract vocabulary, write the words on flashcards so the students can manipulate them.

33. Nonfiction Guided Reading Lesson

Maranda Alcalá
Fairview, Oregon

Recommended Level: Grades 2–3

Overall Objective: To aid students' comprehension of nonfiction books by helping them make connections with the text, work with new vocabulary, and write about what they've learned.

Standards Met (Oregon):

English Language Arts: Use titles, tables of contents, chapter headings, illustrations, captions, glossaries, and indexes to locate information in text; Ask questions and support answers by connecting prior knowledge with literal information found in, and inferred from, the text; Examine content and structure of grade-level informational text across the subject areas; Listen to, read, and understand a wide variety of grade-level informational text including children's magazines and newspapers, dictionaries, other reference materials, and online information

Materials Needed:

- *More Trees, Please!* (Grant, 2008) book—one copy per student
- Notebook paper
- Blank paper

- Chart paper
- Sticky notes
- Index cards
- Brown paper lunch bags

The lesson as outlined will require 40 to 50 minutes each day over the course of approximately five school days.

Day One

Begin the lesson by asking students to sketch a tree. What can you see above ground, underground, in the branches? Try to label as many parts of the tree as possible (without help). Ask the students to share the diagram with a partner. Do they have parts you missed?

Introduce the book *More Trees, Please!* (Grant, 2008). Brainstorm with the students what kinds of information they can learn from the book. Be sure to ask students, "What clues do they have that it is a nonfiction book?" (table of contents, index, subheadings, fact boxes, real photographs, etc.).

Assign each student a section of the book to read silently. Ask them to write the title of their section on a sticky note. Give them an index card on which to write one or two facts from their sections. Make sure students know they will be sharing their facts with the group. When they are done reading, ask the students to share their facts. After each student has shared his or her fact, trade cards with someone else. Now, use the sticky notes with the table of contents headings to sort out the facts. Can they match the fact from the book to the section that it came from?

Read *More Trees, Please!* aloud together. Everyone, including the teacher, reads in unison.

Work together to generate a list of the things that trees provide for us.

Close the group by asking each student to share something a tree provides for us.

Day Two

Begin the lesson by reviewing one of the facts the students learned yesterday.

Next, work on vocabulary boxes. To make vocabulary boxes, take a regular 8.5" × 11" sheet of blank copy paper and fold it into thirds vertically. Then fold the paper in half horizontally. When the students unfold the paper and trace the folds, they will have six rectangles to work with. These are the vocabulary boxes! The vocabulary words for this book could be *sapling, evergreen, deciduous, resource, harvest,* and *forest.* The students write one word in each box, with room for an illustration and a definition (either from the dictionary, the book, or generated by the group).

Reread *More Trees, Please!* aloud together. After you finish the story, ask students to turn to a selected (or assigned) partner to read their favorite part of the story together. This should be short, like one page or section from the book.

Next, ask the students to do a journal entry about what they like to do in or near a tree. For example, students might write about climbing trees or picnicking in the shade of a tree. Give students approximately 10 minutes to write. This journaling does not need to be revised or free from error. It is simply a chance for the students to get some of their ideas on paper. After writing, students can share their writing with the group or with a partner.

Close the lesson by giving each student a question from the book, written on an index card. Ask the students to use the index at the back of the book to determine where they could find the answer to their question. Students can then write the answer below the question or trade questions with a different student and continue to practice using the index to find answers.

Day Three

Begin today by rereading *More Trees, Please!* with a partner.

Review the vocabulary boxes. This can be done as a guessing game or in any other format that is engaging for your students.

Students now will do a quick journal entry entitled "Where is your favorite tree?" Students will need approximately 10 minutes to write out their ideas. This journaling can then be shared with a partner or the group.

Next, use the pictures in the book to make a diagram of a tree. Be sure to include all of the different parts of a tree above and below ground! Students can work in pairs or each make their own diagram. These diagrams will need to be appropriately labeled.

Students can now begin work on a fact-finding activity. One way to organize this is to fold a paper into ninths, due to the fact that there are nine sections in the book (Bauer & Drew, 1992). It could be fewer facts, based on the needs of your students. Have the students search the book for fascinating facts about trees to share with the group. One fact goes into each box. Be sure that the students label each box with the label from the section from the book. The search for fascinating facts can be done individually, in pairs, or in triads.

Close the lesson by asking students to share one of the facts that they read, either with a partner or with the entire group. Students can use the table of contents or index to determine where additional information about the fact could be found in *More Trees, Please!*

Day Four

Begin today with a quick journal entry, "One item from trees I can't live without." Students will need approximately 10 minutes to get their ideas written down. Ask students to reread their writing in a soft voice aloud to themselves to make sure that their writing makes sense. Ask if there are any students who want to share their journaling with the group.

You and the students reread *More Trees, Please!* together. At the end of the reading, ask the students to close their books, turn to a partner, and share two facts about trees (without opening the book!). Ask the pairs to choose one fact to share with the larger group. As the pairs are sharing these facts, ask the students to look at the index of the book. Ask them what section of the book the information came from.

Go back to your tree diagrams from day three. Ask the students to write under each label one or two things people get from that part of the tree. After students complete this additional work on their diagram, ask them to choose one thing that we get from trees. This item will be used for their riddle bag (see Bauer & Drew, 1992). Students will need to draw a picture of their item on an index card and place it inside a brown paper bag. The next step is to write three clues on the outside of the bag that give other students an idea of what might be in the bag. When the riddle bags are finished, students can trade bags and guess what is in the bag. Students can continue trading to continue guessing what is in the different riddle bags.

Close the lesson by asking each student to use the table of contents to determine where the information for the riddle came from. Make sure the riddle bags are returned to their owner before the group breaks up today!

Day Five

Begin today by asking the students, "What facts can you remember about trees?" Write all of their different ideas during the brainstorm on a sheet of chart paper. Use highlighters to label the facts with the different sections from the table of contents. Be sure to talk with students about how the table of contents or index can help them find information in a nonfiction text.

Take a moment to review the vocabulary boxes one last time. How has their understanding of these words changed throughout the study of trees? Ask the students to turn the vocabulary boxes over and write either an original sentence using the words from the boxes or find sentences in the book that use the words. Students can work on this activity in pairs or individually.

Ask the students to reread *More Trees, Please!* independently.

After the students have finished reading the book, they can make a flip-flap book (Bauer & Drew, 1992) about trees. The first step to making a flip-flap book is to fold an 11" × 17" paper into eighths. Next, open the paper and cut on the lines from one of the 17" edges to the fold in the center. This will allow you to lift the flap while still writing information underneath. Each book will have four flaps. The flaps can be labeled "True or False" across the top with a question about trees written just below it. These questions can be taken from the fact boxes in each section of *More Trees, Please!,* or the students can create original questions to ask. On the under side of the flap, students can write whether the question is true or false and give additional information about trees as well. These can be shared with a partner or with the entire group.

Close the lesson today by giving students approximately 10 minutes to journal about the most important thing about trees for them. Remind them to provide justification for their answers. Students can share this journal entry with a partner or with the entire group.

References

Bauer, K., & Drew, R. (1992). *Alternatives to worksheets*. Cypress, CA: Creative Teaching Press.
Grant, K. (2000). *More trees, please!* Chicago: Wright Group/ McGraw-Hill.

▨ 34. Reading Assessment Menu

Reid Nunn
Albuquerque, New Mexico

Recommended Level: Grades 4–5

Overall Objective: To provide opportunities for students who struggle with the verbal/linguistic model, which is heavily relied upon in assessment. The reading menu provides a variety of opportunities using multiple intelligences as well as Bloom's (1956) taxonomy. Students can utilize their strengths in this system to successfully demonstrate their knowledge.

Standards Met (New Mexico):

English Language Arts: Students will apply strategies and skills to comprehend information that is read, heard, and viewed; Students will communicate effectively through speaking and writing

Materials Needed:

- Reproductions of the menu
- Folders
- Tangrams
- Chart paper or large posted notes
- Posted notes
- White drawing paper

Over the years, my students and I have developed activities and assessments allowing opportunities for all learners with varying degrees of higher-level thinking. By the time my students were reaching the fourth or fifth grade, they were tired of the multiple choice or written response forms of assessment. We recognize that traditional assessments rely heavily on the linguistic model, but we felt we could supplement that skill and practice with assessments dealing with the other intelligences.

To begin, we focused on what we felt were the essential standards necessary for a proficient or advanced reader. Currently, education relies upon the verbal/linguistic model to assess performance. We have not eliminated that model from our system, but we have supplemented it with these opportunities. We then used the connections made to create appropriate verbal/linguistic responses in other areas. I began by linking the state standards, multiple intelligences, and Bloom's taxonomy. We focus more on the first three levels of Bloom's taxonomy as we complete our SPECs (summaries, predictions, extensions, and citing evidence from the text) with the reading or audiovisual material. The reading assessment menu pushes the students further into the higher levels of thinking of Bloom's taxonomy. Coupled with Bloom's taxonomy, we incorporated multiple intelligences to allow students to operate within their strengths instead of pigeonholing them into the verbal/linguistic model.

My students and I use this in a variety of ways. One method is to use a 20-sided die. Students complete a variety of activities in their guided reading groups. Every two weeks, they roll the die and complete the corresponding menu item as a group. They then present this to the class. Every group must explain why they focused on a certain section from the novel they are reading. We do this in hopes of the groups determining the essential events within the plot of the novel. They also use their SPECs to give a brief synopsis of the novel and how this activity fits within the plot. This allows groups to model the intelligences as well as proficient comprehension skills for other groups (we usually have four to five guided reading groups). This is also an excellent time to reinforce proficient speaking and listening standards. In addition, we discuss how to ask meaningful and appropriate questions. During independent reading, students choose their own novel and at least three activities within the menu to present to the class.

Students take four weeks to read the novels independently and one week to refine their three menu choices; we then create our own rubric detailing what a beginning, nearing proficient, proficient, and advanced presentation would look and sound like. Students then present their completed projects to the class, and the students grade them. Many students choose to use more than three items to present their novels. Again, students use a brief outline to orally summarize the elements of the novels before giving their presentations. With each activity that they present, they must explain the significance of the event, word, character, or other elements they chose to focus on. An example would be, "I chose to pantomime shooting a bow and arrow because Brian had to use a bow and arrow to kill most of his food." Another example might be, "I wrote a newspaper article about the plane crash because if the plane did not crash Brian would not have to struggle to survive in the woods." We really emphasize the importance of events in relation to the plot of the story. The connections between the menu activity and the text help to make the transition to the verbal/linguistic model.

I require a short, five-paragraph book report outline to accompany the story and to help students organize their thoughts before they present the brief summary. We use the same outline to create five-paragraph book reports as an assessment in guided reading. This also works well with nonfiction reading. An example would be students creating charades for parts of the ecosystem or a cheer depicting important events of the Boston Massacre. In short, this allows students to utilize their strengths and to explore intelligences that are not heavily relied upon in traditional programs. I have found this to be one of the favorite activities of students and have seen some astounding presentations I would not have seen relying upon the verbal/linguistic model of process and product.

Helpful Tips

When introducing this at the beginning of the year, I use reading journals and a data notebook, which contain all the best practice reading tools my students and I have created through the years.

(Continued)

(Continued)

Instead of having students attempt the menu activities early on, as a class, we complete an activity for each section of our guided novels (we break novels into 20 sections). Students complete their guided reading and accompanying activities, and then we discuss the key elements of the menu activity we will complete that day. I complete a shared activity using the shared novel we are currently reading. This models the important aspects and what we are looking for in their guided novel presentations. Students then complete the activity as a group, and we critique the presentations as a class. We use this time to build the concepts rather than to assess. Students take notes right on their menu activity handout in their folder to ensure understanding for future assignments. This does take time, but it helps the students to understand the importance of the connection of the story plot and the activity. This is also a great opportunity to discuss what beginning, nearing proficient, proficient, and advanced products look or sound like. This helps the rubric process progress a bit quicker when you do actually assess the presentations. To practice menu activities, I have also used movies. Compared to written material, the visual comprehension of a story seems to be easier for students to pick. We will frequently reference how we use a certain activity with a children's film and then try and fit the similarities into the story they are reading. For struggling students, I may only require one or two menu choices, depending on their strengths and needs. Students who struggle with written language prefer oral or artwork projects. The system, within itself, is differentiation for all learning models.

Reading Assessment Menu

1. Interview a classmate about how they would change the plot of the story if they were the author.

2. Choose five new vocabulary words from the text, and perform charades for the other groups to guess.

3. Act out a skit of a major event in the story.

4. Pantomime one event from the story.

5. Draw a map of the setting of the novel.

6. Draw a comic strip detailing a major event in the story.

7. Write a song sequencing the major events of the story.

8. Create a cheer describing how the main character plans to solve the conflict of the story.

9. Add sound effects as part of the story is read aloud to the class.

10. Create a Venn diagram comparing and contrasting your actions with the actions of the main character.

11. Create tangrams of a character, animal, setting, or other elements in the story.

12. Create analogies for five vocabulary words for the class to guess.

13. Create a number outline that you can use to represent an event in the story.

14. Outline the main elements of the story.

15. Write a poem describing the main character from another character's point of view.

16. Write a journal entry that the main character would write detailing how they feel about another character or even in the story.

17. Write an acrostic poem using a character, setting, or title of the story.

18. Write a literary review of the story.

19. Create a newspaper article with a picture describing an event in the novel.

20. Write a TV or play script for a major event in the story.

Reference

Bloom, B. S. (1956). *Taxonomy of educational objectives, handbook I: The cognitive domain.* New York: David McKay.

35. Nonfiction Electronic Book

Karen Ann Brown
Littleton, Colorado

Recommended Level: Grades 4–5+, including gifted students

Overall Objective: The objective is for students to get excited about research. They will learn that nonfiction writing isn't always boring and realize how important it is to implement writing crafts in nonfiction writing.

Standards Met (Colorado):

English Language Arts: Students read and understand a variety of materials; Write and speak for a variety of purposes and audiences; Write and speak using conventional grammar, usage, sentence structure, punctuation, capitalization, and spelling; Apply thinking skills to their reading, writing, speaking, listening, and viewing; Read to locate, select, and make use of relevant information from a variety of media, reference, and technological sources; Read and recognize literature as a record of human experience

Materials Needed:

- Research materials from a variety of resources (students' choice)
- Paper
- Pencils
- Computers
- Microsoft PowerPoint

To begin, we read a student *National Geographic*. We listed all the features we could that were (or could be) in a nonfiction book or article. We had a very comprehensive list (see below). Next, we analyzed writing crafts and realized that many of the subtitles were alliterative and found some similes, metaphors, and so on in the articles. Next, we read a variety of other mentor texts to show writing crafts in nonfiction. I showed my students again (I have done this several times this year) how to take two-column notes and the best way to organize them. Students took notes for several days. They had to choose at least 10 writing crafts to use (examples are similes, metaphors, personification, alliteration, one-word sentences, etc.). There are many writing crafts out there, pick the ones you think fit this assignment and make great nonfiction writing.

Student Requirements and Assignment Sheet

1. Write a nonfiction paper (about one to two pages typed) of your choice. Your paper will be your electronic book, except you will be making a few minor changes such as creating hyperlinks, creating a table of contents, and a making a glossary of terms linked to your writing.

2. Include at least four of the following nonfiction features in the PowerPoint presentation.

Writing Craft Cheat Sheet

a. Subtitles

b. Questions

c. Bold words

d. Italicized words

e. Study questions

f. Graphs

g. Maps

h. Captions

i. Cross references

j. Glossary

k. Visual aids

l. Sidebars

m. Bullets

3. Refer to the Writing Craft Cheat Sheet—choose at least 10 of the attached writing crafts.

4. Include Footnotes—use proper format for footnotes, referring to the writing craft used.

5. Use PowerPoint as an effective technological tool to present your information.

6. Cite all sources—books, Internet sites, pictures, graphs, and so on.

Teaching Writing

Overview, Chapters 36–44

36. **Renee Borden,** a kindergarten teacher in Memphis, Tennessee, teaches her students about word and sentence structure by teaching them to write their names in a complete sentence. Each student draws a picture of himself next to their sentence, and the finished pieces are bound together to create a class book. Renee's students love seeing their work in a book.

37. **Nikki Salvatico,** a first-grade teacher from Malvern, Pennsylvania, asks, "What do kindergarteners like to do? They like to talk . . . about themselves." Nikki uses that to her advantage in teaching students about descriptive writing and other narrative techniques. She encourages them to write about themselves, and the stories flow from there.

38. **Kendra Jiles,** a kindergarten through fifth-grade teacher from South Carolina, begins her reading and writing instruction with a bang as students pop balloons to see what their assignment will be. Students create their very own story and use details from that story to complete the assignment.

39. **Karen Ann Brown,** a fourth-grade gifted teacher from Littleton, Colorado, shows her students how to blend genres to create a paper that arises from research, experience, and imagination. Karen lets her student's creativity shine in this multifaceted project that culminates in a class presentation.

40. **Andrea Payan,** an elementary school teacher from Milwaukee, Wisconsin, begins her unit by talking to her kids about their favorite villains in fairy tales and popular movies. Andrea teaches the kids about

154

character development as they design their very own villains to be the protagonists in this creative writing exercise.

41. **Tammy Spratt,** a fifth-grade teacher from Shepherdsville, Kentucky, teaches her class to write feature articles on famous people. The students attach their biographies to cereal boxes, along with vital statistics about the person they chose to research, in a project titled Breakfast Biographies.

42. **Stacy Gardner Dibble,** a fifth-grade teacher from Worthington, Minnesota, uses inquiry to teach her students about memoir. After reading age-appropriate memoirs and identifying the common elements, students try their hand at writing their own memoir. The results are fun and inspiring for all, especially for Stacy!

43. **Kim Tredick,** a fifth-grade teacher from Canyon Country, California, explains to her students that poetry is the best words in the best order. As she reads a passage from *The Borrowers* to her students, they pick out key words from the passage and create a poem from those words. Kim uses this technique in her fifth-grade class, which has a large English language learner population and gifted cluster, and the unit appeals to all.

44. **Sue Davis Pope,** a fifth- and sixth-grade teacher and math coordinator from Provo, Utah, encourages her students to create poems modeled after *Big,* a list of synonyms. Sue's class has fun using their thesauri to make their own poems.

36. Kindergarten Authors

Renee Borden
Memphis, Tennessee

Recommended Level: Kindergarten

Overall Objective: This activity helps students to understand the connection between what is said and what is written.

Standards Met (Tennessee):

Writing: Develop the structural and creative skills of the writing process necessary to produce written language that can be read, presented to, and interpreted by various audiences; Participate in shared writing about social studies, science, the arts, and various classroom activities; Write to acquire and exhibit knowledge (e.g., own name—first and last—letters, numbers); Use appropriate capitalization when writing names; Represent spoken language with illustrations and temporary and/or conventional spelling; Share orally completed work

Reading: Develop the reading and listening skills necessary for word recognition, comprehension, interpretation, analysis, evaluation and appreciation of print and not print text; Read simple text containing familiar letter-sound correspondences and high frequency words; Read some words by sight (e.g., *the, has, an, can, run* and color and number words)

Elements of Language: Use standard English conventions and proper spelling as appropriate to speaking and writing; Form legible upper- and lowercase letters; Use appropriate capitalization when writing names

Materials Needed:

- Large lined writing chart
- Markers
- Scissors
- Glue
- Tag board
- Pointers (for reading)

Developing successful readers and writers is especially challenging for kindergarten teachers. It is so important to provide the rich and varied range of experiences with spoken and written language, which are necessary for oral language and literacy development. This strategy helps to differentiate between letters and words, track print, read from left to right, and practice capitalization and punctuation. Your students will also be encouraged to write and illustrate their own stories at progressive levels of skill and complexity. This activity progresses daily and will take five days to complete.

Day One

This sentence would be appropriate for the first week of school. You will write on the chart "My name is _____" and fill in your name.

You will write this for every student in your class. Each time, I model how to write each sentence by thinking out loud. I write each word and ask students to count the letters in each word, and then we count the number of words in each sentence. I also talk about capitalization and punctuation. I know this seems a lot for the first week of school, but you will be surprised how quickly the students develop an understanding about sentence structure. After you have done this for each student, you will read the chart as a group. As each sentence is read, and the student hears his or her name, they will stand.

Day Two

Using the chart from the previous day, you will read the first sentence on the chart that has your name and model reading left to right and tracking the print. Then read the next sentence, modeling the same procedure, but this time you will not read the name but have the students raise their hands if they recognize their names. When a child recognizes his or her name, have the student to come to the chart and read the sentence. This is a great time to assess students' ability to recognize their names in print, read from left to right, and track print. We need every opportunity to make notes about the progress of our students, so we can plan our instruction to meet their needs.

Day Three

Before group time, I take the chart and cut the sentences into individual strips and ask the children to identify their names and read the sentence to the class. On this day, I again talk about how letters make up words and how words make up sentences. (Teachers, this is where modeling is very important, and you might reconsider ever doing this again, but hang in there, and I promise this activity will help your children acquire important skills in reading and writing.) Take your sentence strip and cut each word into individual cards. After you have cut each word, have the children help you put the sentence back into the correct order. You can use this time to teach the children about correct sentence structure. You then have the students recognize their own sentence strips and cut them into pieces. I do this on the carpet, so I can watch each child cut his or her sentences. I do this step-by-step, so we will not have to write a lot of sentences over. Believe me, over the years, I have rewritten a lot of sentences that were not cut correctly. After the students have finished cutting their words, have them put the sentences into the correct order and read their sentence to the person sitting next to them on the carpet. I then give each student a zip-lock bag for the cards, and they put them away.

Day Four

Teachers, this is my favorite day. I have the students get their bags and put their sentences together on a piece of tag board. You can determine what size works best for you. I take my sentence and glue my word cards on my tag board (at the bottom works best) correctly and draw a picture of myself. I then instruct my students to do the same. This is where I can encourage my students to be creative. I then go around to individual students and ask them to read and track. (Here is another opportunity to assess.)

Day Five

Finally, the finished product and a week's worth of hard work for students and teacher come to life. Prior to group time, I have compiled all the tag board sheets and bound them into our first class book. The looks on the students' faces are priceless when I present their first publication. Each child is able to read, and the year has begun with the children's enthusiasm, wonder, and curiosity about reading and writing. This activity demonstrates a purpose and creates relevance while ensuring that all children acquire the requisite foundational knowledge needed for reading and writing success. Teachers, it is up to you and your creativity on how you wish to use this strategy. I use it often because it gives each of my children the opportunity to participate at their level and be successful. I put these books in our class library, and all of my students can read them independently early in the year. They can take these books home and share them with their families. Also, in the back of each book, I provide a comment page, which provides valuable feedback for me.

37. Teaching Writing

What Works

Nikki Salvatico
Malvern, Pennsylvania

Recommended Level: Grades K–2

Overall Objective: Teach students writing techniques by encouraging them to write about personal experiences.

"I think you should add that!" "What were you feeling when you were walking down the steps to see what Santa had left you?" "Adding more detail, like what color you used to paint your picture, would really help me to create a mental image."

Is this a teacher's dream? No. It's actually what one would hear when walking down the hallways of my school building when passing several kindergarten, first-, and second-grade classrooms. The dialogue above is something I have had the great opportunity to hear over the past few years since I have expanded and revised how I teach writing to my first-grade students.

Many hours of feverishly paging through mentor texts written by such wonderful experts such as Lucy Calkins, Eileen Felgus, Regie Routman, Kathy Collins, Richard Allington, and Debbie Miller, to name a few, has helped me to rethink and plan the delivery and facilitation of teaching writing to my students. In addition, endless collaborative efforts resulting in hours of impromptu book talk in our school hallways, meeting in study groups, and long-cherished phone conversations have also enhanced the continual growth of my ability to deliver what my students need to build their foundation as writers.

When I first began teaching, I remember thinking I had to "tell" my students everything they should do in order for them to be productive and end up with a "choreographed" piece of writing. I use the term *choreographed* mainly because I feel like much of my students' writing in my early years of teaching was guided by my suggestions on what and how to write. I have learned that this technique was very subjective and did not allow for individual creativity, let alone a student's personal growth as a writer tapping into his or her unique gifts, strengths, and talents.

Today, I look at my role as the teacher mostly as my students' facilitator. I believe that handing over ownership to the students creates a classroom environment that invites and flourishes great things, including great writing. This is often difficult for many teachers because it takes away the "C" word . . . *control!* However, I can honestly say, when patience is integrated with enthusiasm and trust, you will see results that will literally blow you away, so you will think you are watching a teaching video from a writing guru's study results—within your very own classroom!

What works? What have I learned? Many things—through experiences that continue to grow me as a writing teacher.

Personal Experiences

What do most first graders like to do? They like to talk . . . about themselves. It is that stage, as Piaget taught us in our early educational classes, the egocentric stage—*it's all about me.* And guess what? It is, and it works! Why not capitalize on a strength they naturally have and is also developmentally appropriate? Students need to write about topics for which they have high interests. Basing writing on past experiences allows students to draw from their own expert schema. Modeling from your own experiences allows for wonderful minilessons that provide the framework for the task at hand. Involving students in sharing their suggestions, thoughts, and questions about the lessons and modeling creates a contagious environment that begins to spark ideas of their own.

Time

Time to write is crucial. I allow about 10 minutes maximum for my minilesson, and then the rest of the hour is used for student writing, teacher-student conferring time, and peer conferring. Consistent, daily writing time is how my students grow as writers. This allows my students to experience, relax, share, and immerse themselves in a writing environment that encourages stamina.

Talk

Talking is something we as teachers are experts at. Not only are we experts at talking, but we tend to enjoy hearing ourselves talk! We love to be the center of attention, the student's focus, the speaker. Bad news: That's not how I run my writer's workshop . . . in fact, it's not how I run any of my teaching, to be perfectly honest. Yes, I talk. I provide the children with minilessons, teacher modeling, and of course reading phenomenal children's literature to demonstrate some of the greatest writers' techniques, but most of the talking is done by my students. Responding to and discussing my examples, the literature examples, and of course the conferring occurs between me and my students, but more important, the "writing talk" occurs student-to-student.

Often, my students will share the most insightful suggestions and ask the most poignant questions that allow a writer to add the perfect details, substituting strong vocabulary, deleting sentences that result in tangent pathways, and providing unconditional supports and cheers for a great job!

Children's Literature

Children's literature is one of the most priceless resources we can use as teachers to demonstrate a variety of techniques to enhance a child's writing. Not only does it allow us to revisit favorite books, authors, and genres multiple times each year but it also allows our students to focus in on parts of stories that demonstrate how to add details that will create a mental image for their readers. It demonstrates how an author can use strong vocabulary, or as Eileen Felgus said in a seminar I took, based on her writing technique, Kid Writing, *million dollar words*. I will take several great books that have rich vocabulary, and instead of having my children memorize chosen vocabulary words, write them five times each, and use them in a sentence, I read, read, and read, focusing on the rich vocabulary, the million dollar words, drawing attention to them. Then, ownership appears again, and I give my students more great pieces of children's literature to explore together in small groups and collect as word detectives—*million dollar words*—for our Million Dollar Word chart. Of course, this chart is available to them at all times, so they can add words as they find them. Ownership, experiences, exploration, discussion, writing: These are the key.

Another way I use great literature is to demonstrate how wonderful authors will begin a story to grab the reader's attention. We then make it our own. Here is an example of Daniel's work after I modeled how to write from a prompt about a favorite toy or food.

Mmmmm . . . mmmm . . . boy do I love faheetahas. They look like a burrito, but they're not. I love them with gwackamoly, salsa, and chees. What I don't like is beans and strained yogurt. I can never eat it all. That means tomorrow, left overs!

Daniel has taken what he learned about grabbing the reader with a great beginning (or as we call them, lively leads), and now he can focus in on his favorite food, describing it with details that create a mental image for the reader, adding feeling and voice to his writing, and leaving the readers with smiles on their faces because they could put themselves inside the story.

Daniel's story went through several steps. He watched and listened to the teacher modeling. He then found a focus for his story, using his schema to add to the content of his writing. He also used fabulous million dollar words that helped to paint a mental image for the reader. He said he did this by using the mental image in his head of when he makes the fajitas at his house for dinner. In addition, Daniel wrote about what usually happens when he eats fajitas and how he feels. It's priceless, original, creative writing. All of the domains of writing are evident in Daniel's writing. He has a focus, with an apparent point made. Voice or style are evident with the use of rich vocabulary and feeling. Organization is clean and clear, using a sequential yet creative format. Phenomenal use of inventive spelling shows evidence of word-family skills; sight-word acquisition is transferred into his writing as well as his knowledge of the conventions.

38. Succeeding With Reading and Writing Instruction for Multilevel Classrooms

Kendra Jiles
Georgetown, South Carolina

Recommended Level: Grades K–5

Overall Objective: To allow students of varying disabilities, ages, strengths, and weaknesses to collaborate on a project demonstrating their knowledge of specific English language arts standards.

Standards Met (South Carolina):

Kindergarten/First Grade: Read and comprehend a variety of literary texts in print and nonprint formats; Learn to read by applying appropriate skills and strategies; Create (first grade will create) written work that has a clear focus, sufficient detail, coherent organization, effective use of voice, and correct use of the Standard American English; Write for a variety of purposes and audiences

Second–Fifth Grades: Read and comprehend a variety of literary texts in print and nonprint formats; Use word analysis and vocabulary strategies to read fluently; Create written work that has a clear focus, sufficient detail, coherent organization, effective use of voice, and correct use of the Standard American English; Begin to write for a variety of purposes and audiences

Materials Needed:

- Chart paper
- Markers
- Crayons and pencils
- Strips of paper
- Balloons

- Multi-color construction papers
- Sentence strips
- Tape
- Stapler

This lesson involves reading and creative writing as the basis for the development of an integrated unit that focuses on many concepts and skills. Students will pick a topic and title, create a story, and use details from that story to complete other activities. This project allows students to create an original story by applying elements of a plot as well as dissect that story for analysis. This project allows those working on all levels of Bloom's (1956) taxonomy to improve their comprehension and writing fluency.

Activity 1

1. Place prescripted prompts into blown up balloons.

2. Assemble students into a circle, and have them pick a student to come and pop a balloon to see what the writing prompt, topic, or title will be.

3. Place large drawing papers on the board with the following headings. Let students name plot elements, and you name the remainder of headings they do not remember. Headings: Setting, Characters, Beginning of the story, Middle of the story, Problem, How problem was solved, End of the story.

4. Students discuss and dictate information to be placed on each chart. There can be more than one drawing paper per heading. Students illustrate pictures to accompany the dictated story.

5. Pages are bound to create a book to be placed in the classroom library.

6. Comprehension questions should now be asked about the story created.

This activity focuses on many concepts and skills. Many times, students have creative ideas for writing stories but lack the ability to develop a story that is coherent and sequential. As students sit around and discuss how to develop the story, cooperation and communication play a major role. Through students dictating sentences, they are able to practice Standard English. The students who will read the story aloud are practicing and increasing their reading fluency. Comprehension questions will range in difficulty according to the instructional levels of the students. The book that is created becomes their published piece. It is also an assessment piece for what was learned and accomplished.

Supplemental Activities: Creation of an Integrated Unit

1. Have students assume the role of the characters or other elements from the story, and have them make a human sequence chain of ordered events.

2. Have students create a tally chart and bar graph pertaining to specific groups in the story—animals, people, places, and so on. Questions pertaining to the graph could be answered.

3. Have students create a list of living and nonliving things from the story.

4. Write a select number of sentences from the story on the board. Take sentence strips and insert them at the end of the sentence. Students expand the story by adding a why or how detail to that sentence. Example: The dog went home *because he heard his master calling.*

5. Place three poster boards on the board with the following headings: Syllable Count 1, Syllable Count 2, Syllable Count 3. Students will locate words from the story and place them on the corresponding poster boards.

6. Create a story quilt. Students write down a detail from the story, along with an illustration, and put them together to make a story quilt.

7. Students may create stick or sock puppets to reenact the story.

8. Take sentences from the story, and within each sentence, have students identify parts of speech.

9. Have students write letters explaining why everyone should read their story.

10. Have students who do not know key words from the story write the words and draw corresponding pictures to help them explain the meanings of the words.

11. Specific words from the story could be used to develop a spelling list for testing.

12. Discuss whether the story is fiction or nonfiction. Ask the students, "What is the difference between this story and another story?"

13. Choose several words from the story, and have students use the thesaurus to find better words to use.

The five big areas of reading are phonemic awareness, phonics, fluency, vocabulary, and comprehension. Activities that were used to develop the unit focus on those reading areas. Activities could be used for individual independent work or cooperative groups. Students' vocabulary would increase through the discussions held. Having a variety of activities allows for movement and for information to be transferred through different means. It also allows activities to be geared toward the interests and strengths of students.

Helpful Tips

Teachers should have topics/titles relating to students' interests as well as those that would allow students to be imaginative and creative. Teachers should also allow students to come up with activities that they would like to do either by themselves or in conjunction with nondisabled peers.

Reference

Bloom, B. S. (1956). *Taxonomy of educational objectives, handbook I: The cognitive domain.* New York: David McKay.

39. Multigenre Writing

Karen Ann Brown
Littleton, Colorado

Recommended Level: Grades 4–5+, including gifted students

Overall Objective: The multigenre paper is an opportunity for students to learn about a famous person, continue to incorporate writing crafts, note-taking, and research skills, and to establish a love of writing in a nontraditional form.

As Tom Romano (2000) states in his book, *Blending Genre, Altering Style: Writing Multigenre Papers,* a multigenre paper

> arises from research, experience, and imagination. It is not uninterrupted, expository monolog nor a seamless narrative nor a collection of poems. A multigenre paper is composed of many genres and subgenres, each piece self-contained, making a point of its own, yet connected by theme or topic and sometimes by language, images and content. In addition to many genres, a multigenre paper may also contain many voices, not just the author's. The trick is to make such a paper hang together. (pp. x–xi)

The following example unit is for a multigenre biography paper. Explain to your students that they will research a famous person/ hero. Encourage them to find information in the biography section of the library. You may want to have your students get their chosen person or hero approved by you before they begin reading and researching. Give them a due date by which they must choose their subjects. Give them a second due date by which to have all of the supplies and books they will need to begin their research, and tell them this will be the first day we will begin working on it in class. Tell them note-taking starts on this day. This unit should take about five weeks. Have your students bring their research materials to school every day.

Following is a list of genres you may want to have your students include in their papers:

- Biographical sketch
- Newspaper article
- Cartoon
- Journal entry
- Letter
- Poem
- List
- E-mail
- Reflection
- Want ad

Inform your students that they can add more genres to their multigenre papers, but these are the minimal requirements. These should be enough to keep the students busy and excited about writing.

Additionally, tell your students that they must have the following writing crafts (Kimball and Swenson, 2005) somewhere in their papers:

- **Five Senses**—Describe, in detail, using the fives senses (Salty waves kept us comfortably cool as the blistering sun beat down upon the outer banks).
- **Show, Don't Tell**—Use vivid details to help your readers see what happens (Her eyes sparkled brightly as she leaped and twirled around the room laughing).
- **Metaphor**—Use metaphor to add texture and tone (The crickets began their melodic symphony as the rays of light melted behind the mountains).
- **Color Words**—Use color descriptions (She entered the room wearing her sunset orange dress).
- **Stretch and Spell**—Stretch words to give them emphasis (Pleeeeease, leave me alooooone!).

- **Sousa Time Word**—Using the setting of the story, the passing of time is shown in a clever way ([at a baseball game] Two hot dogs and a pop fly later . . .).
- **Speaker Tag**—Avoid "he said" and "she said"; use more precise verbs ("Please lower your voice," Kim hissed through her clenched teeth).
- **Repeater Word**—Repeating a word in the middle of a sentence to emphasize a point (Feeling humiliated, all he could do was run, run from all those staring faces).
- **Simile**—Comparing one thing to another using *like* or *as* (The snow covered the ground like the powdered sugar on Grandma's lemon bars).
- **Stand Alone Word**—A single word that stands alone, either before or after a sentence or paragraph, emphasizing a particular point (Nothing. To Pat, nothing was as rewarding as acing the science final test).

Source: From *Weaving "Crafts" Into Writing: Creating a Community of Writers,* by K. Kimball and M. Swenson, 2005, Arvada, CO. Reprinted with permission.

In addition, tell your students their papers must be typed and include:

- Title page
- Prologue
- Genre table of contents
- Writing craft table of contents
- Works cited page
- Pictures—hand drawn, clip art, or photos (your choice)
- Page numbers on each page

Ideas

Students can use special paper that matches their themes. If students or their parents scrapbook, they could scrapbook. Stickers are also another way to add some decoration and creativity to their projects. Help your students make this a keepsake!

Explain to the students that over the next five weeks, minilessons on the above crafts and explicit instructions on the writing genres will be taught in class. Prepare a few multigenre examples to show the class so they know the end result, and have them available at conferences for your students' parents to review as well.

Following the completion of the multigenre papers, have your students give presentations on them over one or two class periods. Encourage them to be creative, to bring music, artifacts, and pictures to add to their presentations. Explain that they will each have about five minutes to present in front of the whole class. Tell them not to read their whole papers but to pick a few of their favorite parts.

Helpful Tips

- One excellent resource is Tom Romano's (2005) book on multigenre writing. Read this book before you begin, and I guarantee you will be excited to have your students write a multigenre paper.
- My students were thrilled to research because they didn't have to write the typical five-paragraph paper or two-page biography; plus, they could be creative and imaginative in their writing.
- Be sure you have previously taught the specific writing crafts you want your students to use (or most of them), and they have had the chance to implement them before expecting them to incorporate them into their writing.
- Rubistar.com has been a good friend to me for many of my projects because I don't have to try and wordsmith every rubric. It's a time-saver!
- As an extension, you can have your students present their newly learned information through a variety of avenues. Their presentations should be creative and exciting. They can bring in music and artifacts, and talk about what they know about their subject. Students can also act like the person and read one or two of their entries.

References

Kimball, K., & Swenson, M. (2005). *Weaving "crafts" into writing: Creating a community of writers.* Arvada, CO.

Romano, T. (2000). *Blending genre, altering style: Writing multigenre papers.* Portsmouth, NH: Boynton/Cook.

40. Creating Villains to Create Great Narratives

Andrea Payan
Milwaukee, Wisconsin

Recommended Level: Grades 4–5

Overall Objective: Students will understand the narrative element of character and how it relates to the plot and themes of a story. Students will produce a narrative piece of writing that demonstrates their understanding of villains and heroes.

Standards Met (Wisconsin):

Reading Content and Performance Standards: Read and respond to a wide range of writing to build an understanding of written materials, of themselves, and of others; Read, interpret, and critically analyze literature. Read and discuss literary and non-literary texts in order to understand human experience

English Language Arts Standards

Materials Needed: A variety of books that can be read aloud that have a strong villain in them. Fairy tales work well for this. Also the Artemis Fowl series of books by Eoin Colfer set up the idea of having the villain be the protagonist.

In creating this lesson, I was trying to come up with a way to get my fifth-grade class excited about writing. This was a group of students that groaned every time the word *writing* was uttered in class. I wanted them to see that writing could be fun, and it could link to their interests. We started this project by thinking about the students' favorite movies. Many students in recent years have been excited about many recently released horror movies. It was easy to steer the conversation to the bad guys in these movies. We started to make a list of the characteristics that these horror movie villains seemed to have in common. We stopped the conversation there the first day. I wanted the students to think about the idea of strong characters and stories in which they are found.

The next few days, I read aloud some books in which there were strong villains and heroes. After we read each story, we went back to our list of characteristics to revise it. We also started to make a list defining characteristics of heroes in our stories. In this way, we were able to focus on the element of character in the story structure. We discussed these characters for a few days. Then, I gave the students the first assignment: I asked them to come up with a villain that would meet the definition that we had come up with in class. They were allowed to brainstorm with classmates, and then they went to work creating characters. I firmly believe that drawing is one of the best forms of prewriting for many students, so they were allowed to draw their characters as well. I was amazed at the level of engagement students had in this task. No one was groaning, and all were enjoying the task of creating a character that would fit within our description of *villain*.

Although most students were happy with this idea, a few students really didn't want to write about a "bad" character. Those students set about creating a hero based on our class definitions. Once everyone had a start on their character, we went back to the books for another look at the story elements. We briefly talked about the plot, the setting, and the themes involved in each story. The next assignment was presented to the students: They were given a story map and asked to outline their story, which would star their villain as the protagonist. When the students had completed the story map, I paired them, so they could give each other feedback. We stuck to relatively simple feedback, which mostly just cleared up any confusion about plot.

Then it was time to get to the writing. The students were enthu-siastic about the writing, and many times they would ask if they could work on the writing throughout other times in the day. By pairing the study of narrative elements with a topic that the students really liked, I was able to bring out a sense of excitement about writing. The quality of writing in the stories was amazing because the students really cared about the topic, and they gave it their all.

HelpfulTips

- I used this activity near Halloween. I do not like to celebrate holidays in my classroom, so this was my way of giving the students a project that they could relate to Halloween if they wanted to.
- This idea could be used with younger students by adapting the ideas slightly to talk about the "bad guys" in fairy tales. They could use the ideas to create a fractured fairy tale in which they make up a character to replace the villain (the Big Bad Elephant instead of the Big Bad Wolf, etc.).
- The same idea could be used to focus on heroes. Students often enjoy creating superhero characters.

---

41. Breakfast Biographies

Tammy Spratt
Shepherdsville, Kentucky

Recommended Level: Grades 4–5

Overall Objective: To introduce students to research and to teach strategies for reading different genres.

Reading is foundational to all subject areas and the success of any child. Therefore, integrating subjects is a critical element to helping students make connections across the curriculum. Teaching students strategies for reading different genres is a must in every classroom, whether you are teaching social studies, science, or math. One way to accomplish this task and meet the needs of the learner is through genre studies. One of my favorite and most effective units of study I do is a biography genre study.

The biography genre unit of study begins with comparing and contrasting biographies and autobiographies. I read picture books about people we have learned about in social studies. We examine the characteristics of the books, and I model reading strategies for reading biographies. I even read excerpts from the encyclopedia about people. We discuss the differences in the reference books and how authors share the life and story of famous people. After reading and modeling, I introduce an array of biographies from the school library and my own personal library.

There is a multitude of biographies available at all reading levels. I work closely with our librarian-media specialist to order new biographies each year. Most school libraries have a larger budget, and the media specialist is more than happy to work with teachers to make sure they have the needed reading material. (Teachers should always keep a list of books and other materials ready. You never know when money will come available.)

Students choose a biography, read it, take notes, and research on the Internet. It helps to give the students guidance and purpose for reading by providing a series of questions. Students want to just give the facts, like an encyclopedia, but I want them to tell the story of a person's life. Therefore, I allow students to write vital statistics and interesting facts about their person, but their feature article must tell the story.

My personal library and our school library offer many choices of historical figures, so that even the most reluctant readers will find a biography that interests them. I encourage the students to become an "authority" on the historical figure of their choice. Choice is one of the keys to success. Several students often pick the same person, and as long as they are motivated to read and research, I am ecstatic. In fact, students with the same person will read different biographies and share their findings with each other, which continues to stir interest and a desire to answer more questions about that person.

After their research is complete, the students write a feature article, with vital statistics such as birth, death, education, and other interesting facts. I integrate technology by having the students prepare a PowerPoint document with pictures and facts. Students use the Internet to find a portrait of their chosen person and glue it on the front of a covered cereal box. One side of the cereal box has "Vital Statistics," the opposite side has "Top Ten Most Interesting Facts," and the feature article is glued to the back of the cereal box; hence the name "Breakfast Biographies."

After becoming an authority on their selected historical figure, I integrate arts and humanities by having students write a monologue and create costumes and props. They present these historical figures in a "Living History Museum" to the students at our school. Students memorize their monologues and use props to enhance their presentation. Students are divided into different genres and stand like statues as if they were a part of a wax museum. The cereal boxes have "red buttons." As the visitors approach the figures, they push the red button, and then the person will "come alive" and tell his or her story. The students speak in first person, narrating a significant time or event in his or her life. For example, Paul Revere may tell about the time he rode through the night to warn the colonists that the British were coming, or Rosa Parks may share how she was arrested for not giving up her seat on the bus. Pocahontas will share about the time she saved Captain John Smith's life, or Ruby Bridges will talk about how it felt as an African American in a white school. Parents and students are invited to the museum and learn about many American heroes. It is one of the most memorable events of the school year.

42. An Inquiry Approach to Writing Memoir

Stacy Gardner Dibble
Worthington, Minnesota

Recommended Level: Grades 4–5

Overall Objective: To teach students about memoir through an inquiry-based approach.

Why choose memoir? Well, in my rush to try something new, I naively picked memoir because Katie Wood Ray (2006), the speaker at a workshop I had attended, included a bibliography of the books she used during her lessons, and I had more of the books on hand that she uses to teach memoir than any of the other units. Decision made. After all, how hard could it be? It turned out to be more challenging than I ever imagined and more rewarding for both my students and me than I ever thought possible.

Immediately, I ran into my first roadblock: What *exactly* is a memoir? How is a memoir different from a personal narrative? An autobiography? If I couldn't recognize a memoir when I saw one, how could I expect my students to understand a memoir, and how would I be able to guide them to write one of their own? Where would I start? I turned to expert writer Lucy McCormick Calkins (1994). In *The Art of Teaching Writing* she has devoted an entire chapter to teaching students to write memoir. It was just the reinforcement I needed to kick off my memoir unit.

I knew it would be a challenge for me to relinquish control of the writing lessons. I was used to teaching my students what a personal narrative or a persuasive paragraph was and what components they would need to include in their own writing. In an inquiry-writing lesson, however, teacher and student uncover the necessary components and flavor of that particular form of writing. Together, teacher and student study many examples of quality writing; they break it apart and discover what makes it a great piece of writing. Once they have those pieces, they use them to form a template to guide their own writing.

To begin, I pulled every picture book from my library that Katie Wood Ray had recommended in her bibliography. Next, I started looking everywhere for short examples of well-written memoir. I decided that I would start this unit in December, after the students had done quite a bit of writing and understood the writing process. This time of year is perfect for memoir because the holidays are a time rich in memories for the students. It is also beneficial for teachers looking to collect examples of memoir for their file. I created a collection of my favorite short passages and made a memoir packet for each student. I wanted students to have exemplary samples of memoir, upon which to model their own writing, at their fingertips.

With great fanfare, we kicked off our unit. I started by reading a few of my favorite picture memoir books to my students. From the moment I read the first memoir, *When I Was Young in the Mountains* by Cynthia Rylant (1982), to my students, they had the task of paying careful attention to the selections that were being read to them. They kept journals about anything they noticed in regards to the way the story is written. I encouraged my students to look at the books and passages as a writer and not as a reader. A writer will look at the book and ask the following questions: What style of writing is this? How did the author introduce the selection? Who is telling this story? What time frame is used? Have I read anything like this before? How does it end?

After the first book was read, we pulled out chart paper and markers and started listing all of the things we noticed about that selection. Then we read another book or passage and repeated the process. This is really where the teacher can lead the students to a better understanding of memoir. For example, my fifth-grade students were bouncing topic ideas around about events that had happened to them just a few weeks ago. Obviously, they did not understand that memoir really needs to be about an event that happened to them when viewed through the window of time. Therefore, we would go back to our examples, and I would ask them, "How old do you think the writer was when he or she wrote this memoir?" "How old were they at the time of the event written about in the memoir?" Then I would use examples from literature to solidify my point.

In this particular case, I went to a great source of memoir: Marlow Thomas's (2004) book, *Thanks and Giving All Year Long*. In it, Tiger Woods wrote a memoir about a coin collection that he sold to help children in Africa. Because he is so famous, it was easy to point out that this was written when Tiger was an adult thinking back to his childhood. Ray Romano has a selection in the same book about a favorite teacher. Both examples helped my students discover that, when they write their own memoir, they need to write about something that happened some time ago. I learned that the more explicitly we talked about the components of memoir—how to start your memoir, what verb tenses will be used, the necessity of sharing how a memory made you feel, and so on—the easier it was for students to write at their age and ability level, and they became anxious to try writing a memoir on their own. Because it has been made so clear to the students what is required when writing in this genre, I really have not had many students claim they had nothing to write.

Once students have started writing, I conference with them. During the conference, I have them read out loud what they have written. I find that students often hear mistakes in their writing better than they can see them. My role at this point is to support my students. This is not the time to take out the dreaded red pen and start imposing your own ideas on their writing. Above all, they need to stay in charge of what is written. This is the time to remind and gently encourage your students to implement all of the writing techniques you have been modeling throughout the year. Every day, there are minilessons for all of the students. The minilessons might be about punctuation or grammar. Sometimes, they are about common mistakes I'm noticing during the individual conferences. Occasionally, you will need to pull your books and great examples of memoir out again to remind your students to use descriptive details or to include more feeling in their writing.

I also ask students to conference with each other. Writing is not a silent time in our classroom. The students have created a writing community, and it is a safe place to try out ideas or word choice with a neighbor. When my student Ethan told about sneaking out to hunt rabbits without his dad's permission he shared, "I climbed the tree nice and quiet. My heart was beating so hard that I could feel it without even putting my hand on my chest."

My students couldn't help but laugh and share with excitement about times when they felt exactly the same way. Every time a student shared a particularly good piece of writing, it inspired the other students to improve their own writing by trying to include a similar tip or strategy.

The last, critical piece of writing memoir is publishing and sharing the students' stories. I have an author's chair, and the students are introduced as if they were a famous, published author on their first Barnes & Noble book tour. They read their memoir to the entire class. The students share what they liked best about that particular piece of writing, and each student's memoir is included as part of that student's writing portfolio.

Since the first memoir unit I taught using an inquiry approach, I have never returned to teaching writing in a traditional style. Every writing unit starts with a crate of books, if possible, a packet of quality examples of the genre I am trying to teach, and a list of minilessons that need to be covered. Each unit is unveiled, and the students could not be more excited to see what it will be about. The students are engaged in the writing process to a level I have never experienced before. The quality of work they produce inspires me every day. The challenge of using inquiry to teach writing is most definitely worth the reward.

Helpful Tips

- Always write along with your students. It makes you more empathetic when conferencing with your students because you have also struggled to do many of the same things you are asking your students to do.
- Writing in front of your students is also a fantastic way to model specific skills for them. It allows them to help you, which improves your classroom writing community. It is also a great way for your students to get to know you better!
- Be on the lookout everywhere for examples of great literature that can highlight any lesson you are trying to teach.

References

McCormick Calkins, L. (1994). *The art of teaching writing.* Portsmouth, NH: Heinemann.

Rylant, C. (1982). *When I was young in the mountains.* New York: Dutton.

Thomas, M. (2004). *Thanks and giving all year long.* New York: Simon & Schuster Books for Young Readers.

Wood Ray, K. (2006). *Study driven: A framework for planning units of study in the writing workshop.* Portsmouth, NH: Heinemann.

43. Found Poetry

Kim Tredick
Canyon Country, California

Recommended Level: Grade 5

Overall Objective: To help English language learners develop literacy and teach all students about symbolism, imagery, and figurative language. To introduce gifted children to the concept *theme.*

Standards Met (California):

English Language Arts: Listening and speaking; Word analysis, fluency, and systematic vocabulary development;

Writing: Word analysis, fluency, and systematic vocabulary development;

Reading Comprehension: Literary response and analysis; Writing strategies

Materials Needed:

- Our current novel, Mary Norton's (1991) *The Borrowers* (any reading material can be used for this lesson)
- Overhead and transparencies (substitute with sentence strips and pocket chart)
- Index cards
- Lined paper
- For our final "published" version, we used construction paper to create layers flowers to have a background for each poem

This lesson was designed as a whole-group open-ended lesson to meet the diverse needs of my fifth-grade class, which includes a large ELL population and a gifted cluster. The technique is called "Found Poetry" and it can be used with *any* reading passage and from second grade and up.

Warm-Up/Introduction

My class has "Coffee House" every Friday morning. We all choose a poem to practice reading all week, and then we read the poem aloud to the class on Friday. I model different types of poetry when I read each Friday. The students have experience with a variety of poetry, and they know that not all poems rhyme. They have an understanding that poetry is "the best words in the best order."

We also are reading the novel *The Borrowers* in literature circles. My lesson objective for Chapters 10 and 11 for the novel is for the whole class to understand figurative language and identifying its purpose. The following examples relate to *The Borrowers.*

Presentation of New Material

1. Reread the descriptive passage of the boy from the perspective of the main character, Arrietty.

2. While reading, record interesting, strong, or emotional words or phrases on an overhead transparency. Explain that selections do not have any criteria except that the choices are personally interesting. For the higher-ability students, I will ask them to identify words or phrases that support and convey the theme of the passage.

3. Explain to the group that these words are the "best words" from this passage.

4. Cut apart the transparency, and on the overhead, begin to arrange the words into the best order to create a free verse.

5. Model thinking about the order of words and phrases, revision of thoughts, adding or changing words for impact, and proper indentation, capitalization, and punctuation for the poem.

6. Create a whole-class free verse rough draft.

7. Reread, revise, and edit the rough draft, and create a final "published" quality poem.

Comprehension Check:

8. Review the steps to create the Found Poem by asking students questions about the process.

9. Have students retell steps to a partner.

10. Reread a paragraph, and ask students to share their choices for best words.

11. Have the students repeat the steps for the process on their own.

Practice

1. Distribute index cards for the students to record their own personally interesting words and phrases.

2. Using the multifunctional cooperative learning structure of "Co-op, Co-op," in which the ELL students work in pairs, have the students read aloud and record their own choices on the index cards.

3. Ask that students work independently to create their own special free verse rough draft.

Evaluation

1. Create a "published" version of their poem.

2. Celebrate the completion of the poem and the students' ability to be successful poets.

3. Create a display product of the poems to be posted on the wall of the classroom.

Helpful Tips

- Model! Model! Model! When creating the class poem, rearrange phrases, repeat phrases and words, talk about making changes for impact, edit and revise punctuation, ask students for assistance, and accept all suggestions when recording words and phrases.
- You can make this lesson as simple or as complex as the kids you are serving. You can change the level of the novel, have students all use their own independent novels, use a grade-level anthology, or utilize another poem as the basis material. You can also use this same strategy and change the focus of the standard to fit your grade level, such as finding powerful verbs for third grade.
- I have also done this lesson both with whole class and small groups. The discussion of word choice and placement is important. Talk with the kids as they create and rearrange, to explore their understanding of the word choice. What I most like about

this lesson is that all children are successful, no matter their level of English proficiency, intellectual capabilities, or writing abilities. They all produce products that I am proud to display every time.

Reference

Norton, M. (1991). *The borrowers*. San Diego: Harcourt Brace Jovanovich.

44. The "Big" Poem

Sue Davis Pope
Provo, Utah

Recommended Level: Grade 5

Overall Objective: After reading and analyzing the poem, students will successfully use a dictionary and a thesaurus to find synonyms of a descriptive word of their choosing and create a poem using the author's craft of organizing the synonyms by gradients of meaning and numbers of synonyms or syllables.

Standards Met (Utah):

Vocabulary; Writing: all objectives

Materials Needed:

- Overhead of poem for shared reading
- Writing materials
- "Big" by Colin McNaughten (1994) from *Making Friends With Frankenstein*

I introduce the poem "Big" by putting a copy on the overhead. I cover the text but expose the title. I have students predict what the poem is going to be about. Based on past experience with reading poetry, my students make and explain their predictions. We read the poem together from the overhead, with my voice taking the lead. We discuss together what this poem is—a listing of synonyms.

We read and discuss each line, trying to see if we can find a pattern to the author's choices of why he listed specific words where he placed them. Some students recognize that there is semantic gradient of meaning, and others notice number of words and/or syllable patterns. I define and emphasize the semantic gradient of meaning because I think it is the most enriching and interesting aspect of the poem. We count the words in the poem together and find that the poet used 26 synonyms.

We talk about where they thought a poet would come up with so many words that mean close to the same thing. We discuss the skill of how to use a dictionary and a thesaurus. Students quickly come to recognize that there are not enough words when simply looking up the original word. They have to use the synonyms they find in the reference books and look those up as well.

Using Vygotsky's (Pearson & Gallagher, 1983) theory of "Gradual Release of Responsibility" and author's craft, we write a poem together. We decide what our topic word will be and look up the word in the dictionary and in the thesaurus. We list the words we find, and look those up as well, until we have a few more than 26 words. Then we discuss the semantic meanings of the words and decide which ones belong together. Using the poem as our guide, we discuss, negotiate, decide, and "share the pen" while we create a poem together.

Next, they collaborate in small groups to write another poem.

At this point, most students are comfortable with the procedures and expectations, and each student writes his or her own poem independently. They all work through the writing processes as they draft, revise, edit, and publish.

References

McNaughton, C. (1994). *Making friends with Frankenstein: A book of monstrous poems and pictures.* Cambridge, MA: Candlewick Press.
Pearson, P. D., & Gallagher, M. C. (1983). The instruction of reading comprehension. *Contemporary Educational Psychology, 8*(3), 317–344.

PART IV

Teaching Social Studies, Music, Art, and Physical Education

Teaching
Social Studies

Overview, Chapters 45–51

45. **Christopher R. Shadle**, a third-grade teacher in Massillon, Ohio, invites students to think about the culture they grew up in relative to other cultures around the world, past and present. The students celebrate their unit with a "feast fit for a king" where they use a mock passport to travel between other countries to learn about different food and fairy tales.

46. **Kim Heckart**, a third-grade teacher in Cedar Rapids, Iowa, teachers her students about prejudice against African Americans during the time of segregation. Her students learn about Jim Crow laws and sharecropping through literature, photos and documents from the time period, and making timelines.

47. **Karen Ann Brown**, a fourth-grade gifted education teacher from Littleton, Colorado, asks students to report monthly on current events around the world. In this unit, Karen teaches her students about the world in relation to themselves, other current or historical events, and cause and effect.

48. **Luella L. Atkins,** a reading specialist in Berkeley, Missouri, introduces her class to presidential inaugurations through a study of the poetry read at four inaugurations. Luella encourages students to think about the individual elements of the inaugural ceremony and they get to plan their own inauguration.

49. **Heather E. Robinson**, a fifth-grade teacher from Scottsdale, Arizona, believes in taking social studies off the shelf and bringing it to life in the classroom. Heather has students sit two to a chair to model the Quartering Act and she decorates her walls with propaganda posters such as "The King's Gotta Go!" during their study of pre-Revolution America.

50. **Eileen Biegel**, a fifth-grade teacher from Orange Park, Florida, takes her students on field trips to study local history through architecture. Eileen's students experience first-hand the work of historians and they make real-life connections to history in their surrounding community.

51. **Tammy Spratt**, a fifth-grade teacher from Kentucky, demonstrates the experience of immigrating to the United States through Ellis Island by having the students simulate the experience. Acting as the immigration agent, Tammy marks the students as ready for immigration or needing further inspection as they learn about the real-life trials of many immigrants through various fiction and nonfiction sources.

45. Cultural Diversity in Our Community

Past and Present

Christopher R. Shadle
Massillon, Ohio

Recommended Level: Grades K–4

Overall Objective: To help students become more aware of cultural diversity in our world and how diversity can achieve unity. This was an all-school project integrating social studies with language arts for the students of a K–4 Building.

Standards Met:

National Geography Standards: Study how culture and experience influenced people's perception of places and regions; Study the processes, patterns, and functions of human settlements; Study how to apply geography to interpret the past

Ohio Standards:

Citizenship: Compare some cultural practices and products of various groups of people who have lived in the local community, including artistic expression, religion, language, and food; Compare cultural practices and products of the local community with those of other communities in Ohio, the United States, and countries of the world; Describe settlement patterns of various cultural groups within the local community

Geography: Identify and describe the landforms, climate, vegetation, population, and economic attributes of the local community; Identify ways the physical characteristics of the environment have been affected and modified by the local community

History: Define and measure time by years, decades, and centuries; Place local historical events in sequential order on a timeline; Describe changes in a community over time, including changes in businesses, architecture, physical features, employment, education, transportation, technology, religion, and recreation

English Language Arts and State Standards in Citizenship: Acquisition of vocabulary; Reading applications of informal, technical, and persuasive text; Writing applications, the writing process, writing conventions, research, and oral and visual communication

Materials Needed: Artifacts from other cultures, books about other cultures including fairy tales, and food from other cultures. These items may be obtained from your local and school community.

The project "Cultural Diversity in Our Community: Past and Present" involved the entire school community with assemblies and an ethnic fair called "A Feast Fit for a King." The assemblies for the school included a presentation on Ancient Egypt and King Tut presented by the Canton Cultural Center; a Native American who shared song, dance, and stories with the children; performers demonstrating European dancing;

and a steel drum performance with African dance. These activities were arranged to help students to become more aware of cultural diversity in our world and how diversity can achieve unity.

During this project, the third-grade students of our school studied communities around the world, including customs and traditions as well as learning about communities of the past. The thematic unit covers a three-month period. In the unit, the children study how our country developed from the earliest settlements of the Native Americans, explorers, colonists, and pioneers. The students study cultures around the world, as well as communities of the past, in order to gain an appreciation of the heritage of our country. Through integration and the various learning channels, the children learn about the past and other cultures through the "hands-on, minds-on" approach of learning by doing. They compare some cultural practices and products of various groups of people who have lived in the local community, including artistic expression, religion, language, and food. They also compare cultural practices and products of the local community with those of other communities in Ohio, the United States, and countries of the world, and they describe settlement patterns of various cultural groups within the local community.

Initially, the children of our school visited the Massillon Museum, our local community museum. Through a scavenger hunt, the children were able to locate and observe artifacts of the Native Americans at the museum. In addition, the students learned about the diverse cultures and various industries that established the community of Massillon. The students visited Schoenbrunn Village, a community founded in 1772 as a Moravian mission to teach the Delaware Indians; Zoar Village, a village founded in 1819 by the Germans in order to establish a better way of life and to worship God in their own way; Hale Farm and Village, a community located in Northeast Ohio, gave the students another perspective of an early settlement; Spring Hill, which is a local historic site in Massillon, Ohio, was built in 1821 and served as a stop for the Underground Railroad. Through visiting these historical sites, the students were able to compare and contrast the cultures, the various reasons why people came to the New World, and where, why, and how they settled in the New World.

During the project, the children wrote and illustrated books about the way they envisioned life of the past. Daily lessons were presented to the children in a variety of ways, through books, historical inter-preters, storytelling, slide presentations I developed, and videotapes. Together, we explored archaeologists and historians, the Native Americans, the Vikings, explorers (Marco Polo, Christopher Columbus, and Amerigo Vespucci), the English and the Pilgrims, the French, the Spanish, and slavery. Using technology, the students also located information and researched a country of their choice in order to gain knowledge of another culture for their book. They were able to see the effort people put forth in order for our nation to develop. This expe-rience developed the children's expository writing abilities, preparing them for achievement tests.

The children then created a mural and used scenes from their books to illustrate a timeline of our country, including the Native Americans, explorers, early colonists, and the pioneers who settled here in Ohio. Through Venn diagrams, tables, and charts, the children were able to compare and contrast cultural communities.

During their studies, the students created a chart with three columns listing things they knew (K), what they wanted to know (W), and things they learned (L), the KWL Chart. With 80% accuracy, the students listed three facts for each of the columns and it was evaluated using a four-point rubric. This chart was one product indicating what they learned about the various cultures.

Pretests and post-tests are another way to indicate what the students learned. I use pretests and post-tests to measure achievement and a rubric to evaluate the books, reports, and displays for this project. Written reports, books, and oral presentations were measurable instru-ments to indicate meeting the objectives. As I taught about communi-ties, I taught about communities of the past, communities around the world, and local communities. I had to adapt my lessons to meet the needs of the age groups of my students, and I included the "special needs" students in all activities.

The first activity was an archaeological dig where the students found artifacts and had to identify the artifacts and their uses. This activity integrated the science processes into the lessons, and they began to use those same processes to problem solve in the other disciplines as well. The students learned how the pioneers and Native Americans used natural resources in order to survive and make products. The students made pinch pots out of clay as the earlier cultural groups did in order to make utensils to survive. The children were able to design watercolor paintings of artifacts they observed at the museum. Each child had the opportunity to weave a scarf on a loom. This process gave the students an appreciation of the effort it took to make a finished product from long ago. In addition, the children experienced a quilting bee as the pioneers as well as other cultures experienced. Each student designed a square to illustrate his or her vision of the early settlers. All the children helped sew the quilt together. The children also designed model ships like those used to travel to the New World. The pupils designed models of the various kinds of shelters used by the various culture groups that settled in the New World.

The third-grade students from our school partnered with a third-grade class from another school to study culture groups in Ohio and around the world. The children were able to compare and contrast the reasons why the cultural groups came to settle in the New World. The children researched information, developed reports, and made displays of the cultures they studied. A culture exhibition was held at our school district's central office. The children dressed in costume, and their displays included food and artifacts from the cultures researched.

The 21st Century After-School Program collaborated with the day school at L. J. Smith Elementary School in this project, learning about various cultures around the world. The teachers incorporated the cultures and fairy tales in their lessons at all grade levels. The after-school children were able to experience the various assemblies through video. In addition, the after-school children participated in activities during "Right to Read" week.

This project was integrated with our Right to Read week. Each grade level selected a fairy tale associated with a country or culture. The grade-level teachers engaged their classes with a variety of activities focusing around fairy tales and the cultures they came from. The grade level was responsible for developing a display including the fairy tale and their country or culture, food, and a craft or activity. The culminating activity was the all-school ethnic fair, "A Feast Fit for a King." At the feast, the students of our school visited other country displays to learn more about cultures around the world by using a passport as they traveled from place to place.

Each grade level presented activities, maps, and information for the children. They could travel to Norway to sample gingersnaps and make a flag of the country. Then some were off to England to have some tea and biscuits and try to see if they could blow a piece of straw, wood, or brick across the desk as the wolf did in "Little Red Riding Hood." Others went to China to sample a fortune cookie and try to pick up food with chopsticks. Yet others went to Germany to try bratwurst and make a cuckoo clock. Some went to Italy to try some pizza and help make a tower of Pisa out of marshmallows. As a culminating activity, The Cultural Diversity Right to Read week began with a kick-off assembly on fairy tales presented by the teaching staff of the school through "Reader's Theatre." The Right to Read week included activities throughout the week: Read a Shirt Day, DEAR (drop everything and read) Time for 15 minutes, Royal Hat Day, Fairy Tale Trivia, Read a Button Day, Dress as Your Favorite Fairy Tale Character Day, and the culminating activity, the ethnic fair, A Feast Fit for a King. In addition, we had paired reading where children from various grade levels came together to read to the younger students; they kept a daily reading log and were able to play on a Fairy Tale Room-Sized Game Board. The Fairy Tale Room-Sized Game Board was located on the stage in our gymnasium. The object of the game was to answer trivia questions related to fairy tales and move from the Enchanted Forest to the Magic Castle.

The funds for this project were provided through grants from The National Geographic Society Education Foundation, The Ohio Arts Council, and L. J. Smith Elementary School Parent-Teacher Organization.

Helpful Tips

Planning ahead is the key in order to obtain grants and resources for the project. This project was made possible by the collaboration of the entire school staff. Careful planning and scheduling is required in order to make this project a success.

46. Prejudice Against African Americans During the Time of Segregation

Kim Heckart
Cedar Rapids, Iowa

Recommended Level: Grade 3

Overall Objective: To teach students about Jim Crow laws and give them a historical perspective about racism and prejudice against African Americans.

Standards Met (Iowa):

History: Students understand how democratic values came to be and how they have been exemplified by people, events, and symbols.

Social Studies: Time, continuity, and change; Individuals, group, and institutions; Power, authority, and governance

Materials Needed:

- Jim Crow laws
- Copy of the Fifteenth Amendment (available at http://www.loc.gov/rr/program/bib/ourdocs/15thamendment.html)
- 1965 Voting Rights Act (available at http://www.usdoj.gov/crt/voting/intro/intro_b.htm)
- *Goin' Someplace Special* by Patricia McKissack and Jerry Pinkey (2001)
- *Papa's Mark* by Gwendolyn Battle-Lavert (2003)
- *A Homesteading Community of the 1880s* by Gare Thompson (2002)
- KWL (What I know, What I want to know, What I learned) chart for photo analysis
- Historical photos of Jim Crow laws and sharecropping
- Photo links for the third-grade segregation unit (available at www.bringinghistoryhome.org)

This is the fifth lesson in a unit on slavery and segregation. In this lesson, students identify prejudices against African Americans shown through Jim Crow laws and sharecropping. Prior to this lesson, students have studied slavery, have been introduced to the Civil War, understand the Constitution is a document that is the set of rules for the United States, and know that the Constitution can be amended, such as with the Bill of Rights and the Thirteenth Amendment that stated "No more slavery."

Day 1

To hook the kids, say, "Has anyone ever called you a name or been mean to you? On the count of three, tell a shoulder partner how that made you feel." Then have some of the kids share how they felt with the whole group.

Next ask, "What does Jim Crow mean?" If kids do not know, I define it as "a derogatory term for African Americans and was originally a song title. *Derogatory* is like calling someone the meanest name that you can think of. We know how it feels to have that happen. When slavery ended, many white people in the South didn't want it to end, so they started Jim Crow laws. Jim Crow laws made it so African Americans didn't have the same rights as white people. I'll read some of the Jim Crow Laws to you."

We discuss what they mean.

Next, I put students into groups of four. Each group gets a historical photo to analyze (the students are not told what the photos are, but each group has a different photo representing a Jim Crow law), a KWL (What I know, What I want to know, What I learned) chart for recording information about the photo, and a pencil. In their small group, students number off one to four. Ones start as recorder while the other group members are contributors. The recorder fills out the first section of the KWL chart, People, as the contributors tell the recorder what to write. The recorder writes what everyone says even if they don't think it is a correct answer. The recorder may also write what he or she thinks. When their section is complete, the recorder passes the paper to the group's two to take over as recorder. This will continue until the entire paper is complete. It is a way to make everyone in the group accountable. When I give each group a photo, I do not give any background about it; instead, it is a time for them to dig deeper into the photo and see if they can figure out what is happening. When each group finishes, they come back to the rug area with their KWL chart and photo. Each group shares their KWL chart and shows their photo to the rest of the class. As each group finishes their sharing, I post their photos and KWL charts on a big piece of paper, and the kids come up with a title for it. As they begin to see all the photos, they realize all of them are examples of Jim Crow laws.

I have a second copy of each of the photos, and we add those photos to our classroom timeline. The timeline runs from the 1600s through the present. Our timeline is a visual representation of what we learn throughout the year. It is not a list of dates to remember, but it is instead a way to understand chronological and cause-and-effect relationships between events. In the course of the school year, it becomes a tool students use to infer when something happened by deducing where it might belong on the timeline.

Finally, I read aloud *Goin' Someplace Special* (McKissack & Pinkey, 2001). Students listen to the story and give a thumbs up when they hear me read about a Jim Crow law in the book.

This leads us to defining two words, *segregation,* to separate, and *prejudice,* judging another by their outside and not considering the person on the inside. I explain that the era of the Jim Crow laws was a time called segregation because whites established ways to be separated from African Americans. White people were showing prejudice against African Americans.

Day 2

I read the Fifteenth Amendment to the students: "The Fifteenth Amendment of the United States Constitution provides that 'No government in the United States may prevent a citizen from voting based on that citizen's race, color, or previous condition of servitude.' It was ratified on February 3, 1870."

What does this mean in third-grade words? "African American men can vote." (Girls will question immediately, "What about women?" I say, "Yes, at this time women couldn't vote, and it didn't matter what color their skin was. There is an amendment that does allow them the right to vote. See if you can do some research and bring it to school tomorrow." The next day I always have students ready to share about the Nineteenth Amendment.) In 1865, African American men were given the right to vote, but many white people did not want them to vote. I introduce the next book (Battle-Lavert, 2003) by saying, "Listen while I read this story, *Papa's Mark,* to find out what white people did to try and stop them from voting." I always read the author's note because it gives a historical account that summarizes what we've learned in our whole unit on slavery, the Civil War, and the Fifteenth Amendment. After reading the book, I share the 1965 Voting Rights Act. We discuss how President Johnson finally makes the literacy tests and poll taxes illegal. We add the 1870 Fifteenth Amendment note card and the 1965 Voting Rights Act note card to our classroom timeline. When the kids see the note cards on the timeline, they realize it is almost 100 years before African American men may vote.

The students are then given a writing assignment: "Pretend it is 1964, and write a letter to persuade President Johnson to stop this problem of African Americans not being able to vote."

Day 3

Ask, "Has anyone ever heard the word *sharecropping*?" I have found this is a new word for children. We start by breaking the word into parts: "What does *share* mean?" (Children are good at giving examples of things they share and who they share with.) "What is a crop?" (Because we live in Iowa, students can easily talk about corn and soybean crops grown here.) "What was one of the main crops grown in the South?" (cotton). I tell the children that another way that people were kept from having equal rights was by sharecropping. "After slavery ended, many freed slaves couldn't afford to buy their own land, so they went to work in the cotton fields for men who used to be slave masters. They had to 'share' the money they earned with the landowner. This caused African Americans to be very poor because they could not get ahead when they had to give half or more of what they earned to the landowner. I'd like to read chapters one and two from *A Homesteading Community of the 1880s* (Thompson, 2002) about a family that this happened to. Listen carefully to the story, and see if you can make any connections to other stories we've read in this unit."

Next, put students into groups of four, giving each group a historical photo that relates to sharecropping (again, I do not tell students what the pictures are; it is their time to investigate). They fill out their KWL chart as they did in the previous part, and share their findings with the whole class. It is a quick assessment to see if the kids understood what we discussed about sharecropping. The photos can easily be confused for the time of slavery. In our sharing time, we discuss how this is sharecropping, but it looks like slavery. I ask, "Why do you think this is?" It leads to a discussion on how sharecropping and Jim Crow laws were ways that white people didn't allow African Americans to have equal rights. It was a time of prejudice and segregation.

After this lesson, students will learn about African American people who resisted segregation and what life was like from 1865 to 1950.

HelpfulTips

From 2002 to the present, I have participated in a Teaching American History (TAH) Grant project in which I teach, adapt, and create lesson plans for social studies and history units. The segregation lesson I describe in this article is adapted from a unit that is part of that TAH program, the Bringing History Home curriculum. The curriculum includes five instructional strategies that can be used with all grade levels. The strategies are geographic mapping of historical content, analyzing photos and documents, using literature for background content knowledge, creating timelines, and using synthesis projects to culminate student learning. Bringing History Home lessons for grade levels K–5 are free for public use and are available at www.bringing historyhome.org.

References

Battle-Lavert, G. (2003). *Papa's mark.* New York: Holiday House.
McKissack, P., & Pinkey, J. (2001). *Goin' someplace special.* New York: Atheneum Books for Young Readers.
Thompson, G. (2002). *A homesteading community of the 1800s.* Washington, DC: National Geographic Society.

▨ 47. Current Events

Learning About Our World

Karen Ann Brown
Littleton, Colorado

Recommended Level: Grades 4–5+, Gifted

Overall Objective: To help students stay up to date on current events, help them become familiar with the newspaper and various other nonfiction resources, improve comprehension, and increase confidence in public speaking.

I usually introduce this unit by talking about what is going on in our world, how we find information, and how important it is for us to be informed. I have organized this several different ways. Students report monthly; I usually assigned certain days for each student. Originally, I had students present every week but found that the quality of the assignment went down, and so did the motivation, plus it was a nightmare getting 28 students to present every week. Presenting monthly worked out well. Have one kid present a day, perhaps first thing every morning.

Many years ago, Pearson Education (Pearson, 2000–2008) came out with a event map (graphic organizer), which I use specifically for this assignment. Students are expected to complete the organizer and complete a typed paper using the information from the organizer. Students must include the following in their paper and speech. First, students need to write a summary of an important event including the who, what, where, when, and how. Next, they draw a map of the setting where the story took place. Third, students then discuss cause-and-effect elements of the story. Fourth, they must compare this event to another event (which doesn't have to be current). Fifth, they need to make a prediction as to what they think will happen next and support their opinion with facts and information from the text and their own background knowledge. Last, students need to discuss their own personal reaction to the event—how this event makes them feel and why. Again, it's all about supporting their opinion.

Short version

1. Summary

2. Setting (drawing)

3. Cause/Effect

4. Comparison—This is similar to . . .

5. Prediction—What do you think will happen next?

6. Personal Reaction to the event

I was amazed by the intensity of some of these articles and the effort and work students put forth. This was a very worthwhile and engaging assignment.

Helpful Tips

- Model a few times for students before expecting them to complete the parts of the assignment on their own.
- Let the students' first time through the assignment be a practice one, so you can discuss the *dos and don'ts* of presenting.
- Include self-assessment each time.
- Use a rubric to assess, and be sure students know exactly how they are being assessed.

(Continued)

(Continued)

- The rubric should include written as well as presentation skills.
- If I strictly used the newspaper, I had students pick different sections from it. For example, if they picked an article from the sports section one month, they could not do it again and would have to pick an article from government and politics, editorials, movie and book reviews, science, education, or another section. If I didn't organize it this way, I would have certain students (usually boys) who would always complete an article from the sports section.
- In addition, with the younger students, some parents were concerned about their child reading really sad or scary news and didn't want them to be frightened. Of course, I let the parents make that final decision, but all students still had to complete the assignment using each section of the paper at least once.

Reference

Pearson Education. (2000–2008). *Event map.* Author. Retrieved May 5, 2009, from http://www.teachervision.fen.com/journalism/graphic-organizers/2279.html

48. Inaugural Poetry Through Elementary School Publications

Luella L. Atkins
Berkeley, Missouri

Recommended Level: Grades 4–5+

Overall Objective: To introduce students to presidential inaugurations through a study of inaugural poetry.

Standards Met (Missouri):

Communication Arts and Social Studies: Read, view, listen to, and evaluate written, visual, and oral communications; Use a variety of strategies to interpret texts; Read, view, and listen for specific purposes (such as scanning to find needed information); Read, view, listen to, and recognize a variety of literary genres; Apply prior readings and experiences to aid comprehension; Recognize and understand figurative language (such as personification, simile, and metaphor)

Materials Needed (select only two poems):

- Copies of Miller Williams' poem "Of History and Hope"
- Copies of Maya Angelou's poem "On the Pulse of Morning"
- Copies of Robert Frost's "The Gift Outright" and "Dedication"
- Copies of Elizabeth Alexander's "Praise Song for the Day"

Inaugural Poetry

Four times in U.S. history, poetry has been read at presidential swearing in ceremonies. Robert Frost read his poetry for John F. Kennedy in 1961. Bill Clinton asked Maya Angelou to read her work for his 1993 inauguration. In 1997, Clinton again asked a poet, Miller Williams, to read for the inauguration. Like Clinton, Williams is an Arkansas native. And in 2009, Elizabeth Alexander read for the inauguration of Barack Obama.

Robert Frost certainly reflected Kennedy's background of New England pride and prominence. By asking Angelou to read, Bill Clinton started his presidency speaking to the power of diversity and inclusion in a true democracy.

A side note: Robert Frost actually wrote "Dedication" for John F. Kennedy's swearing-in ceremonies. When the sunlight made it difficult for Frost to read his poem, he recited a poem he knew by heart, "The Gift Outright."

All of these poems are beautiful works of art, but they have also become political documents, speaking to specific moments of time in the United States.

Overview

Presidential inaugurations have been solemn ceremonies and uninhibited celebrations. They are carefully scripted, and they are unpredictable. They reflect tradition, and they reflect the moment.

Guiding Question

What is required by the Constitution to occur at a presidential inauguration? What other events occur or have occurred at inaugurations?

Procedures

1. Discuss the history of poetry at U.S. presidential inaugurations.

2. Distribute poems.

3. Organize students into small groups, or differentiate assignments based on ability or interest, asking each group to discuss and analyze one poem.

4. Each group must select a recorder, passage picker, reporter, timekeeper, and facilitator.

5. Ask each group to answer, in writing, some or all of the following questions.

6. Discuss the questions and answers after the group work is complete.

    a. How does this poem reflect the times during which it was written?

    b. How does the poet make us think about the past? How does the poet make us think of the future?

    c. What are the poet's dreams for the future? Cite examples from the poem.

    d. Cite any examples of personification. How is personification used in each poem?

7. After students have completed this assignment, ask one member of each group to read the poem aloud.

8. Another student from each group should paraphrase the group's discussion of the poem.

9. During the whole-class discussion, each student should take notes using the three-minute format (McTighe & Lyman, 1988): (1) summarize key ideas, (2) adding his/her ideas, and (3) posing clarifying questions.

10. Repeat steps 3 through 9.

Tiered Assignments

1. Ask students to write a poem that will inspire America as well as speak to the country's past and future.

2. Ask students to find another poem that would be appropriate for an inaugural ceremony. Students could memorize the poems and then recite them in class.

3. Should the event focus only on the Oath of Office, the pledge to preserve, protect, and defend the Constitution?

4. If students could organize the inauguration, what activities would they continue to have?

5. Who would students invite to their party?

6. Would they invite the candidate who lost?

7. Ask students to explain why they made the choices they did.

Reference

McTighe, J., & Lyman, F. (1988, April). Cueing thinking in the classroom: The promise of theory-embedded tools. *Educational Leadership,* 18–24.

49. How Simulations and Impersonations Inspire Students

Heather E. Robinson
Scottsdale, Arizona

Recommended Level: Grade 5

Overall Objective: To make history relevant and fun for students through simulations and impersonations.

Standards Met (Arizona):

> Students understand the development of American Constitutional democracy grew from political, cultural, and economic issues ideas and events; Regional conflicts led to the Civil War and resulted in significant changes to American social, economic, and political structures; The U.S. structure of government is characterized by the separation and balance of powers

Taken as a whole, the teaching of history, geography, and civics has been given a raw deal. This most naturally captivating subject area has been turned into an uninspiring and often tedious subject for students to learn about, and for many educators, to teach. My overall objective is to create inspired learners who can't believe they once thought social studies was a dull and unimportant subject area.

Social studies is a subject often overlooked in classrooms, primarily because standardized or statewide testing is lacking. This, in turn, makes it the subject teachers feel they can gloss over in order to give "testable" concepts more time. I'm fully aware of the pressure we're under to fit everything in, but I refuse to abandon effective social studies practices by simply "covering" material. Providing creative ways to integrate social studies is not only possible but also energizes the whole classroom!

In order to make the best use of my school day, I integrate history with the primary subjects. Reading is a natural fit. For instance, when we are learning about the Revolutionary War, our literature study is a historical fiction book that takes place during that time. By overlapping subject areas, a wealth of facts is introduced, and the students have a familiarity with the topic from both ends. I don't always relate a literature book with the social studies unit—kids need exposure to genres other than historical fiction—but it does show the difference a good literature book can make in understanding history topics. Writing is the ultimate way to express ideas learned about any subject. With various simulations taking place within the main unit, writing assignments are certain to be enhanced as the students reflect upon their new experience.

Take the Quartering Act of 1765, forcing colonists to give food and housing to soldiers. To introduce this concept, I tell the class they must sit two or three to a chair for the duration of the current activity—for instance, while going over vocabulary words. At first, the novelty of it wins out, and they enjoy their close quarters. After about ten minutes, however, they wonder when they can return to their own seats. Once we move to social studies, and begin talking about the meaning of the Quartering Act, the purpose of being seated so strangely dawns on them in an "aha" moment, and writing comes easier. They have a reference point because they are still simulating the lack of personal space. This idea sticks with them, and they write naturally with voice and creativity. Math and geography offer the opportunity to work with population growth, graphing, and mileage between colonies, in addition to countless other activities. There are wonderful connections to other subjects as well: decorating the room with propaganda posters such as "The King's Gotta Go!" and playing music indicative of the time period being studied, as they work on activities, brings in art and music.

The reason that simulations and impersonations work so well with social studies is because securing the knowledge of history, geography, civics, and other components of citizenship applies to all of us. Although ideas described here apply directly to American history, any area of social studies is ready to be simulated. One of my students' favorite impersonations of the year is when we learn about the three branches of government, and the students portray government employees. I remember an individual telling me that it's impossible for elementary students to understand the government because her high school students have such difficulty with it. When parents visit to witness a "Typical Day in Washington, D.C." during our *Three Branch*

Dress, it's obvious that these fifth graders are well aware of how government functions. Limited expectations from others just inspires me to continue the path I'm on and has motivated me to invite others to join the fun. Two of my teammates have adapted my ideas in their own classrooms with complete success.

All students should regard learning as the fascinating adventure it is, and they should take the opportunity to embrace it. My motto is clear: Take social studies off the shelf, and bring it to life in the classroom!

HelpfulTips

- Don't be afraid to create your own path. Traditional textbooks are good resources but are often boring, or conversely, jammed with so many sidebars, biographies, and trivia that they cease to be as effective. Ask yourself, How would I like to learn if I were sitting in the classroom?
- Participate in and attend state or national social studies related conferences. Teachers provide the bulk of presentations, and many creative ideas are at your fingertips.
- Utilize Web sites, such as www.gilderlehrman.org, that give you access to primary documents from the Gilder Lehrman Institute of American History. They also provide an online history journal, *History Now,* with lesson plans and other information.

---

50. Archi-Techs

Learning U.S. History Through Architecture

Eileen Biegel
Orange Park, Florida

Recommended Level: Grade 5

Overall Objective: Upon completing this project students will be able to use technology to summarize specific events in U.S. History.

Standards Met (Florida):

Social Studies: Time, continuity, and change; People, places, and environments

Technology: Creativity and innovation; Communication and collaboration; Research and information fluency; Critical thinking, problem solving, and decision making; Digital citizenship; Technology operations and concepts

Information Literacy: Accesses information; Evaluates information; Uses information; Pursues information; Strives for excellence; Recognizes the importance of information; Practices ethnical behavior; Participates effectively in groups

Materials Needed:

- Digital camera(s)
- Digital video camera
- Printer
- Scanner
- Computer
- Audacity software (free download available) for recording podcasts
- Photostory for creating vodcast documentary
- Notebooks for recording sketches and notes
- MP3 player for recording notes during field studies
- Flash drive
- Belkin microphone for MP3 player
- Construction materials for scale models of buildings

"Archi-Techs" is a project-based multimedia learning experience in which students examined the essential question: If buildings could talk, what would they tell us about the past? Technology and architecture were integrated with the content areas of social studies and language arts during this yearlong study of U.S. history. Acting as archi-techs, fifth-grade students learned U.S. history through a study of local architecture and national historic buildings within the surrounding counties. Students learned the basic elements of architecture and simple geometric principles of design and how the early settlers in Florida used available materials to design buildings and homes to meet their needs and acclimate to their surroundings. The classroom was extended to the outside community through a partnership with local architecture firms, historical societies, and the National Park Service. Students interviewed local architects and historians, and they utilized the historical archives to examine primary sources, such as deeds, to research the history of the featured buildings and homes.

The first field study was a walking tour of historic St. Augustine, Florida. The purpose of this field study was to complement the background knowledge the students had acquired in their social studies classes. The students were assigned an "Archi-Techs Quest" (scavenger hunt) in which they had to answer questions or draw buildings or architectural details based on clues about the buildings. They spent the day exploring, documenting, and listening to the stories and history of specific buildings in St. Augustine. The locations included Castillo de San Marcos, the Oldest House (Gonzalez-Alvarez House), Flagler College (formerly Hotel Ponce de Leon), St. George Street, the Plaza, Lincolnville (the house where Martin Luther King Jr. stayed during the civil rights movement), and Old St. Augustine Village. Student teams listened to historians describe the buildings and their stories, and the students documented their visit through photographs and field notes.

An additional mini field study was scheduled for the town of Green Cove Springs. The students explored the downtown area and learned the rich history of this quaint town located on the St. Johns River. Since we are limited on the number of field trips that we can take students on each year, I brought historic places to the class through "virtual field trips." For example, I visited the Kingsley Plantation, in Duval County, and shared video and photographs in my class. I also supplemented this virtual field trip with information from the National Park Service Web site.

Armed with this new information, student teams conducted additional research at the school media center about the buildings, including their history, interesting stories, and architectural features. This research was used for the students to "interview" the building to give a perspective of U. S. history as seen through the buildings of the past. Next, they created storyboards and show notes (scripts) about their assigned buildings. The students practiced their scripts and created "first person" podcasts, in which the buildings told stories and history from the building's perspective. These podcasts were available on a Web site for families and friends to listen to.

The culminating activity for this project was the creation of a vodcast documentary to summarize what the students learned. In addition, student teams created a scale model of each of the featured buildings and houses. The scale models were placed in a chronological timeline in the media center. A student-hosted gathering was held where parents, administrators, our architectural and historical partners, and members of the local community viewed the multimedia documentary and visited the architectural timeline of U.S. history.

"Archi-Techs" is different because it is an opportunity for students to learn "outside of the book" and experience the work of historians. It allowed students to make real-life connections to history and their surrounding community instead of passively reading about it in a textbook. Students saw a reason to do this project. History came alive for the students as they were engaged in this hands-on project.

Helpful Tips

It would be beneficial for teachers to create their own podcast prior to introducing this tool to their students. There are many Web sites available to learn this process.

51. Immigration

Was *Your* Name Changed at Ellis Island?

Tammy Spratt
Shepherdsville, Kentucky

Recommended Level: Grade 5

Overall Objective: For students to understand why people come to America today compared to why people came to America long ago.

Standards Met (Kentucky):

Social Studies, Grade 5: Use a variety of primary and secondary sources (e.g., artifacts, diaries, maps, timelines) to describe significant events in the history of the United States and interpret different perspectives; Explain reasons (e.g., freedoms, opportunities, fleeing negative situations) immigrants came to America long ago (colonization, settlement, industrialization, and immigration—20th century to present) and compare with why immigrants come to America today; Describe significant historical events in each of the broad historical periods and eras in U.S. history (colonization, settlement, revolution, and a new nation, expansion and conflict, industrialization and immigration—20th century to present), and explain cause and effect relationships

Materials Needed:

- Teacher-created PowerPoint that includes primary sources (Google image search for *Ellis Island* and/or *immigration*)
- Photographs and other primary sources from Ellis Island for each student
- Copy of manifest from Ellis Island
- Large letters representing the different medical problems faced at Ellis Island
- The book *Journey to Ellis Island: How My Father Came to America* by Carol Bierman (1998)
- Hats and props representing different cultures for students (hats are a great way to teach history. I collect them from the Goodwill and yard sales)
- Music CD "Where Are We Going?" from *Tunes That Teach American History* (Sheldon, 2005)
- 12" × 18" construction paper for each student
- Questions for cooperative groups (families for simulation)
- Examples of primary and secondary sources
- *If Your Name Was Changed at Ellis Island* by Ellen Levine (1993)

Historical Perspective

History is an account of events, people, ideas, and their interactions over time that can be interpreted through multiple perspectives. In order for students to understand the present and plan for the future, they must understand the past. Studying history engages students in the lives, aspirations, struggles, accomplishments, and failures of real people. Students need to think in a historical context in order to understand significant ideas, beliefs, themes, patterns, and events, and how individuals and societies have changed over time in Kentucky, the United States, and the world.

Essential Questions for the Unit of Study

- Why are people willing to leave their homeland and come to America?
- What was life like as an immigrant? Who are immigrants today?
- How do primary sources help us to learn about the past?
- Where are we going, and who will we be?
- Was your name changed at Ellis Island? Angel Island?

Procedures

1. Project images (primary sources) of immigrants at Ellis Island. Have students imagine being one of the immigrants. Play the song "Where Are We Going?" from *Tunes That Teach American History* (Scholastic, Ken Sheldon, 2005) while the images are projected on the screen from the PowerPoint. Students view the primary sources and listen to the words. Pause, reflect, and discuss the kind of feelings these immigrants may have been experiencing. Help students make connections with the experiences that the family has in the book, *Journey to Ellis Island: How My Father Came to America* (Bierman, 1998).

2. Summarize the first, second, and third chapters from *Journey to Ellis Island: How My Father Came to America.* (Note: A chapter a

day is read from this book, based on a true story, written by Carol Bierman, the granddaughter of the main character, Rachel. Also, during Language Arts, students will be reading an informational book called *If Your Name Was Changed at Ellis Island* by Ellen Levine, 1993, providing background knowledge before the simulation.)

3. Read chapter four, "Twice Around the Island: Ellis Island, September 1922," and have the students imagine coming to America and having to experience the physical examinations immigrants faced upon their arrival.

4. Share the objectives for the lesson.

5. Review the difference between primary and secondary sources. Confirm students' recollection of this concept. Share the copy of a manifest from Ellis Island, and ask whether it is a primary source or secondary source. Share other examples, and have students identify them as either as primary secondary sources. Explain that they will be previewing several pictures (primary sources) from Ellis Island.

6. Explain to the students that they are going to travel back in time and "experience" what it may have been like to come to America through Ellis Island.

7. Divide the class into small groups and assign roles: mother, father, children, grandparent, and so on. The group will be given a list of role cards to prepare for the simulation during the legal exam simulation at Ellis Island.

8. Students will choose a hat and a prop to help them play the part of immigrants.

9. Share the chart (primary source) posted at Ellis Island. You can make a chart with the different chalk markings inspectors used at Ellis Island or get the image from the Internet and have it on PowerPoint. (During the medical exam, for example, an immigrant's shoulder was marked in chalk when the inspectors/examiners suspected a problem.)

10. Line the students up in the hall with their "families" and their props, and have them assume their assigned roles.

11. The teacher will assume the role as an examiner/inspector at Ellis Island, dressing for the part as well.

12. Direct students to walk into the "Great Hall" and prepare for questions and examinations.

13. Role play medical examiner and mark the students with large letters and send some to the detention centers for further examinations; allow others to continue the process through Ellis Island. The teacher will also ask many questions and pretend to log the information on a manifest. Eventually, the students will be allowed to come to America.

14. Afterwards, a debriefing session will begin. The teacher will ask a series of spiraling questions, allowing time for reflection of the experience.

15. Chorally read the words to "Where Are We Going?" from *Tunes that Teach American History* (Ken Sheldon, 2005), and discuss their meaning. Play the song again and sing along with students.

16. Each student will then receive several pictures (primary sources). They will create a picture collage using primary sources and create speech bubbles. In the speech bubbles, students will reflect their feelings as well as factual information. Review how to draw and use speech bubbles. The following are content words to be used at least once in the speech bubbles:

Buttonhook	Statue of Liberty	Trunk
The Great Hall	Better way of life	Land of the Free
Freedom	Chalk letters	Medical examiners
Examination	Detain	Passport
America	Land of Plenty	Language
Trachoma	Inspectors	

17. Students will also have a homework assignment and write a letter, using the content words, to someone in their homeland describing the experience of coming to America.

18. The following day, the images will be displayed and students will act out the scenes.

Optional Activities and Extensions

- Play the song "The Great American Melting Pot" from School House Rock (Newall & Eisner, 2002).
- Read *Immigrant Kids* by Russell Freedman (1995).
- Research the Statue of Liberty.
- Review other primary sources and "Evaluate that document!"
- Read stories about present day immigrants.
- Research the laws for naturalization.
- Research family trees.

Make a copy of the role cards for students to use when working in their cooperative groups to prepare for the simulation:

ROLE CARD

Roles: father, mother, children

Name of country/nationality?

Age, gender, marital status, occupation

Destination, who paid for the voyage?

How much money do you have?

Names of relatives in the United States

What will the family do if one or more are detained at Ellis Island?

HelpfulTips

When teaching the unit of study on immigration, or any unit, it is important to have a question, title, and organizer that promote thought and reflection. This lesson is called, "Was *Your* Name Changed at Ellis Island?"

References

Bierman, C. (1998). *Journey to Ellis Island: How my father came to America*. New York: Hyperion Books for Children.

Freedman, R. (1995). *Immigrant kids*. New York: Puffin Books.

Levine, E. (1993). *If your name was changed at Ellis Island*. New York: Scholastic.

Newall, G., & Eisner, M. (2002). *School house rock* [television series]. Burbank, CA: Walt Disney Video.

Sheldon, K. (2005). *Tunes that teach American history*. New York: Scholastic.

Teaching
Music, Art, and
Physical Education

Overview, Chapters 52–56

52. **Heather E. Robinson,** a fifth-grade teacher from Scottsdale, Arizona, enhances her social studies curriculum through a study of historical music. Students have fun singing songs from the Civil War and enjoy listening to the tones of traditional Native American music.

53. **Denese Odegaard**, a string specialist from Fargo, North Dakota, invites her students to celebrate their musical talent by hosting concerts for their families to enjoy. Denese incorporates world foods into a concert of music from around the world and uses an Academy Award–themed concert to honor students with awards.

54. **Susan Menkes,** an elementary school art teacher in Jericho, New York, tracks student progress from K–sixth grade by keeping self-portraits students draw at each grade level. When students graduate from elementary school, Susan awards them with a collection of their self-portraits.

55. **Cindy L. Hodgeson,** an adaptive physical education specialist from Tucson, Arizona, has created a Motor Lab in addition to the regular physical education kids receive in elementary school. Cindy knows that the physical strength and flexibility students acquire at a young age can effect their ability to learn, and she wants to see all her students learning to their full potential.

216

56. **Tammy Haggerty Jones,** a third-grade teacher from Saulk Village, Illinois, describes a few activities that will get students' blood flowing and make them better behaved and better learners in the classroom.

52. Celebrating Music

Heather E. Robinson
Scottsdale, Arizona

Recommended Level: Grades 4–5+

Overall Objective: To enhance the social studies curriculum through the use of music.

Standards Met (Arizona):

Music and Art: Art in Context: The student will demonstrate how interrelated conditions (social, economical, political, time, and place) give meaning to the development and reception of thought, ideas, and concepts in the arts

Diverse Functions of Music: The student will discuss diverse functions that music serves

Art as Inquiry: The student will demonstrate how the arts reveal universal concepts and themes; Students reflect upon and assess the characteristics and merits of their work and the work of others

Describes Ways Music and Other Disciplines Relate: Students will describe ways in which subject matter, principles, and other disciplines taught in the school are interrelated with music

Thoroughly engrossing kids in what they're learning about is much easier when it's supplemented thematically. As experienced teachers know, children readily welcome related topics, and enjoy natural relationships between the subject areas.

One of my favorite methods of enhancing each social studies unit is through the use of music. The rich music of this country is familiar to everyone, and, with the Internet, quite easy to locate and play. My students love the fact that music enters into the regular curriculum in addition to the official music class.

When we're learning about Native Americans, we learn verses from indigenous songs. The music connection, however, centers around the playing of Native American music, so students can hear traditional instruments and tones. After the social studies lesson, as the kids do their independent work, they are also hearing the beautiful sounds of this culture. Songs of early America are very easy to incorporate, especially because they're often played around the holidays. We play "We Gather Together" when learning about Pilgrims before Thanksgiving. When my students are learning about the era around the American Revolution, they sing "Yankee Doodle" if they're in the Patriot group and "God Save the King" if they are a Loyalist. Although this lesson plan concentrates on a single social studies unit, it's easy to see that music is adaptable to any part of history as well as to other subject areas.

Short List of Civil War Songs

Union	Confederate
"Battle Hymn of the Republic"	"Dixie"
"Battle Cry of Freedom"	"Bonnie Blue Flag"
"Union Dixie"	"Goober Peas"
"Yankee Doodle"	"When Johnny Comes Marching Home"

Helpful Tips

- Determine which songs you'd like your students to learn. It's important to expose the children to songs sung by both Union and Confederate sides.
- Civil War song CDs are great to have, especially for playing in the background, but are not the only source for music. Nearly any song you want the kids to learn is available on the Internet. There are numerous Web sites (for example,

http://www.pdmusic.org/civilwar.html) available. Also, by Googling *Civil War songs* or a specific title, it's easy to find any song.
- When locating songs on the Internet, the lyrics are sometimes written on that page. If the classroom has a PowerLite projector or the computer is hooked to the TV, the kids can read the words right off the screen. Otherwise, just print the lyrics for them.
- In addition to the traditional Civil War songs most of us are familiar with, a nice touch is to teach the students some of the humorous ones. For example, "Dixie" is a popular Southern song, but the Union soldiers created their own lyrics to that same tune, and students really get a kick out of it (especially if it's introduced after everyone is secure with the Confederate version).
- During an art connection to the Civil War, or other activity that doesn't need complete concentration, use Civil War music in the background. When songs they recognize play, the kids will sing along, and have fun with it.
- Some songs have many verses. Pick out no more than two verses for the students to master. Learning too many from one song might be hard to accomplish, and it's fun for the kids to be familiar with a variety of melodies.

53. A Taste of Music

Concert Ideas

Denese Odegaard
Fargo, North Dakota

Recommended Level: Grade 5

Overall Objective: To celebrate students' musical abilities by holding themed concerts for their families and the community.

Standards Met (North Dakota):

Music: Students understand music in relation to history and culture

Scheduling concerts a year in advance around theater productions, holidays and days off from school, and other music concerts and activities is sometimes difficult. The only date I could find for my fall concert was a Friday, which is not the best day for families.

We decided to make it appealing, so we added traditional hors d'oeuvres from other countries. We started the event around 5:30 p.m., with a concert following the hors d'oeuvres.

We chose music from all nationalities and invited parents and area restaurants to contribute finger foods. Our English as a second language (ESL) students and foreign language teachers brought decorations or helped with the decorating. Olympic flags sewn by students a few years ago hung around the cafeteria. I bought some colorful plastic tablecloths and paper place mats that transformed our cafeteria into a festive restaurant

Here are the partnerships that developed:

- Parents
- Area businesses (don't forget to thank them in writing)
- ESL students/foreign language teachers

It was nice to have the ESL students involved in this concert because they felt another connection to the students at school and were able to share their culture with others.

Parents of students new to our school started the year with a positive experience and were able to become involved right at the start of the year. Students also had time to socialize before and after the concert, during set up and clean up.

Academy Award Concert Theme

Select movie themes and make it an Academy Award–themed concert. We had hors d'oeuvres before the concert, found a red carpet to put at the entrance of the school, and had limo companies donate free limo rides before the concert.

This was our last concert of the year where we present awards, so we incorporated this into the award idea.

We had a master of ceremonies from the local TV station introduce pieces, and for each piece we had pictures or film clips or poster images projected on a screen, using PowerPoint.

We traced and cut out several eight-foot Academy Award statues and spray painted them gold and hung them around the cafeteria during the hors d'oeuvres. For a "Walk of Fame," we cut out stars, mounted them on black paper, and wrote the name of each orchestra student on them and put them in a row across the front of the stage.

Companies that donated pizza, soda, limo rides, and red carpet had ads in the program.

Winter Wonderland

For a winter theme concert we hung snowflakes from the catwalks, so they hung above the audience, stuck glow-in-the-dark stars on the sound shell, and purchased artificial snow to "snow" from the catwalks. We put the snow in several shoeboxes, poked holes in the boxes so that the snow could fall out the bottom, and lined students up on the catwalk to shake the boxes during "Winter Wonderland." It had a great effect!

54. Progressive Portraits

Susan Menkes
Jericho, New York

Recommended Level: Grades K–6

Overall Objective: This project will develop a sequential and reflective learning experience for your students; show and measure actual individual growth and development; create extremely meaningful, easily doable one or two 40-minute lesson plans; and wow parents. Your students will gain a new perspective of themselves by recognizing their year-by-year development. They will realize through their progressive portraits their physical changes, cognitive development, and improved drawing ability. This will lead the way for meaningful self-reflection in a final written assessment when students are able to see all their portraits side by side.

Materials Needed:

- 9" × 12" white drawing paper or 8 ½" × 11" computer paper (Tip: Be consistent, using the same size of paper year after year, in order to mount all the portraits together with ease.)

- Pencils, pens, colored markers, crayons, oil pastels, water color paint, tempera paint (Tip: The medium you offer your students is up to you. I usually begin with crayons in kindergarten and offer more engaging and age-appropriate materials as the students get older.)
- Mirrors (Tip: I have invested in large plastic stand-up mirrors that are available in all the arts/crafts catalogues. However, if your budget doesn't allow for these, small glass mirrors can be found for a reasonable price at the "99 Cents" stores. Tape the edges and backs of glass to prevent their chipping and breaking.)
- Manila folders—one for each student (Tip 1: Using a colored marker, write the name of each student on the tab of the folder. Use a different color marker for each grade level. For example, write all the names of the kindergarten students in red, the first graders in orange, the second graders in yellow, and so on. Tip 2: As each class graduates and you empty the folders, cross out the names and reuse the folders the following year for the incoming kindergartners.)

Background: Each year, the New York State Art Teachers' Association has an annual conference with a variety of presenters who share their expertise with fellow art teachers. The progressive portrait idea was first introduced many years ago at our state conference by Jessica Bayer. I have put my own "spin" on it. Although I rarely repeat lessons year after year, this is the one lesson I do as an annual end-of-the-year finale. My students anticipate these portraits with excitement and they have become the highlight of fifth-grade graduation. Most important, it is a project that my visiting high school seniors tell me they have kept and will continue to cherish.

The appropriate grade levels for this sequential learning experience are kindergarten through sixth grade, or whatever grade levels you teach in your elementary school. The lesson meets all four New York State visual arts standards, as well as the national standards for the visual arts.

Process: Students create a self-portrait each year that I file away and reveal to them upon their elementary school graduation. Make sure your students sign and date their portraits every year with their grade level. In the weeks before graduation, the portraits that have been saved in each student's folder are mounted side by side on long strips of paper. This is an easy way to display all the artwork on graduation day.

An important part of the process is a written assessment. I ask my students to express in writing how they feel when their progressive portraits are finally revealed to them after six years. Questions I ask them include, "How do you think you have developed as an artist?" "What changes have occurred since you were in kindergarten?" and, "What memories of your years in elementary school are evoked from these pictures?"

55. The Motor Lab and Sensory Tools for the Classroom

Cindy L. Hodgeson
Tucson, Arizona

Recommended Level: Grades K–4

Overall Objective: To improve student focus by allowing students to exercise.

Standards Met (Arizona):

Physical Education: Students demonstrate proficiency and develop an understanding of skills necessary to enhance motor skills; Students comprehend basic physical activity principles and concepts that enable them to make decisions, to solve problems, and to become self-directed learners who are informed, physically active participants; Students exhibit a physically active lifestyle; Students develop self-initiated behaviors that promote personal and social interactions in physical activity settings

Materials Needed:

- Balance beam
- Teeter balances
- Rocket launchers
- Ball pit

- Wands
- Mini trampolines
- Floor mats
- Balls (playground balls, tennis balls, punch balls, inflatable balls)
- Jump hoops
- Jump ropes
- Hula-hoops
- Twirl and jump (made from ball, stick, and rope)
- Skip and hop (made from rope and ball)
- Elastic bands
- Flip and catch
- Duck walker (quantity 4–6)
- Bungee jumper
- Scooters
- Plastic domes
- River rocks
- Spinning boards (Quantity 4–6; do not use Sit-N-Spin; use Spinning boards ordered from Ready Bodies, Learning Minds, www.readybodies.com)

In our school district, I have initiated a "Motor Lab" that provides all kindergarten through fourth-grade students the opportunity to address reflex integration, sensory needs, and motor development to enhance learning. The Motor Lab is different than PE, with more structured individual and partner activities to specifically enhance learning readiness. Motor Lab is in addition to the school physical education program.

If you have been an educator for some time, you are probably aware that expectations have changed academically, and students entering school seem to have more issues than in the past. Many students are entering the school system with neurological systems that are not ready for learning. With this current generation, many kids are playing video games, watching movies, on the computer and Internet, and are not outside running around as much as in the past. In addition, the academic expectations in our schools have risen, and students are required to sit and learn more and produce more, at a much younger age. Many students are entering our classrooms with sensory needs and are craving movement. I believe these students are often misdiagnosed as ADHD, as they have to be up and moving and have difficulty focusing without the extra movement. In addition to "the mover," aka, "the bouncer," there are children who can't seem to make it through the day without propping themselves up or the opposite, slumping in their chair and on their desk, aka, the "noodle." The third type of sensory child we all have seen in our classrooms is the "chewer," who has to have something in his or her mouth, usually a shirt! All of these students need extra sensory input. What can we do to help them function in our classrooms in a productive way?

In addition to the sensory system is our reflex system. There are four primitive reflexes that we are born with and should be integrated by age two. Research shows that if these reflexes are not integrated by the time a child is in school, the child can or may experience academic difficulties, and it will have an effect on learning readiness (Blythe, 1996). These reflexes include the asymmetrical tonic neck reflex, symmetrical tonic neck reflex, and the labyrinthine reflex, supine and prone. All of these reflexes, if not integrated, can affect handwriting, crossing the midline, catching, posture, and coordination. As teachers we need to be aware of the "total package" we are receiving at the beginning of the year and try to understand better the "root" of behavior and learning.

With all that said, how can we address all these needs? You can make a difference and begin to utilize sensory tools in your classroom as well as initiate a Motor Lab in your school. Seem impossible? It can be done! I would like to give you information and activities to get you started on the right path to providing opportunities for your students to improve their learning readiness. I know we all want our students to be successful!

Let's begin with the Motor Lab. I would highly encourage every teacher to attend the Ready Bodies, Learning Minds workshops (http://readybodies.com/component/option,com_events/Itemid,26/) that are held all over the country, which give you a wealth of information, in much more detail than I described, on how learning is affected by neurological development and the sensory system. It was through this workshop that I learned how to begin a lab in my school. In the two elementary schools in my district we have the Motor Lab up and running. All students, kindergarten to fourth grade, attend the lab at least one time a week, with kindergartners attending two times a week. Half of a class attends at one time, with the other half remaining in their classroom, then they switch. When the students enter the Lab (which is a classroom turned into a Motor Lab) they begin their reflex exercises as a group on the mats. Next, the Motor Lab assistant or myself explain briefly the stations the students will be doing that day. The stations remain in place for two weeks and are then changed. Students rotate with a partner to each station, usually two minutes a station, to complete designated challenges. The session ends with a tactile activity such as a "ball massage," where students relax and lay on the mats while their partner uses a playground ball to apply deep pressure across the legs, arms, and back. When students leave the lab and return to class they are calmer and more organized through the movement opportunities provided. The total time for each session in the lab is 20 to 25 minutes. Note that this is in addition to, not in place of, regular physical education classes in our district. Depending on your state or district, you may or may not have PE on a regular basis. Either way, this program is beneficial!

In our Lab, stations are posted on the wall along with the warm-up reflex exercises and cool-down ball massage. Activities are divided into the following categories, with a specific progression within each category: proprioception, eye-hand-foot, motor planning, tactile, vestibular, balance, ball workout, and locomotion. All activities for these areas are available through the Ready Bodies, Learning Minds Web site, in the activities book. See my own example of an activity included in our Lab that fits in the balance category (river rocks), at the end of this section. Notice that the plan includes what specifically the child will do, performance objectives, and further suggestions for success. Each plan or activity lesson included in the *Ready Bodies, Learning Minds Activity Guide* has those three items included and makes it very easy to follow.

To purchase materials for your lab you can try several options. In our district, we have an educational enrichment foundation, parent teacher group (PTG), and school tax credit monies available. Our current Labs were funded through our enrichment foundation and PTG.

Additional sensory tools for the classrooms were funded through an award from ING Unsung Heroes. The materials for the lab are numerous with some items being handmade and others purchased through US Games (http://www.usgames.com/), Sportime (http://www.sportime.com/), and S&S Worldwide (http://www.ssww.com/sports-pe-recreation/). There are many grants available online, and with persistence you can acquire monies to make your Motor Lab happen! You will need approximately $2,500. This includes two mats, a ball bag ball pit, four spinners (which look like lazy susans), and all other items needed. You can get away with a smaller cost factor with more items being handmade.

The Motor Lab is one way to provide students the sensory input, reflex integration, and motor development activities they need. In addition, I want to encourage you to include ball chairs in your classrooms because ball chairs are a great way for your bouncers and movers, low tone kids, and those who have difficulty focusing to get the extra movement they need during class time. We have incorporated over 65 chairs at each school, and have one classroom using ball chairs exclusively for all the students in that class. The response from classroom teachers has varied, with the majority of teachers seeing the chairs make a positive difference with students. As with all things, not every tool works for every child. There have been a few cases where the child needed "limited" time on the chair due to too much stimulation or movement, and some children cannot use them at all.

Some teachers have opted to use the chairs just at their reading stations or just for specific activities in class. Specialists have also requested chairs for their rooms, such as our speech teacher, special education teachers, reading specialist, and occupational therapist.

After much investigation, we have found the ball bowls or stands with a 55 cm therapy/exercise ball sitting in it to be the most cost efficient and practical ball chair for our students.

Another sensory tool that we utilize in many of our classrooms is to incorporate Bal-A-Vis-Xs (http://www.bal-a-vis-x.com/) into the daily routine. Bal-A-Vis-X was designed by Bill Hubert, and is a program that utilizes beanbags and balls in rhythmic patterns while balancing on a board. There are over 300 patterns and tricks to learn. Bal-A-Vis-X stands for balance, auditory, and vision exercises. It helps students cross the midline, improve auditory processing, improve eye tracking (which helps in reading and writing), and improves focusing and concentration

B a l a n c e

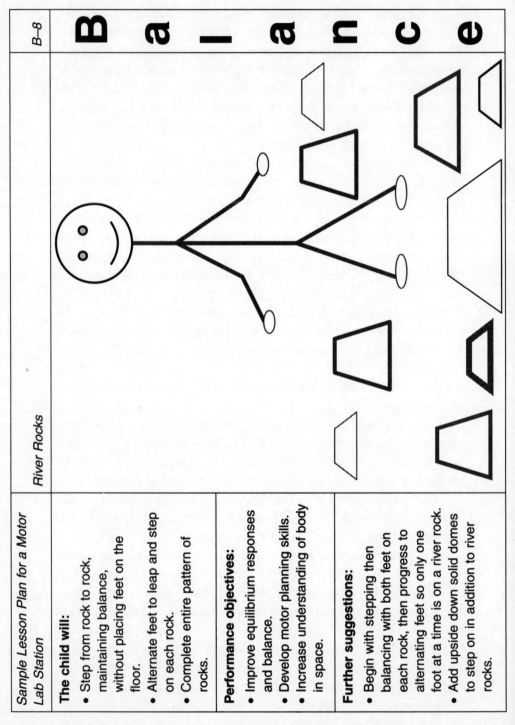

Sample Lesson Plan for a Motor Lab Station

River Rocks

The child will:

- Step from rock to rock, maintaining balance, without placing feet on the floor.
- Alternate feet to leap and step on each rock.
- Complete entire pattern of rocks.

Performance objectives:

- Improve equilibrium responses and balance.
- Develop motor planning skills.
- Increase understanding of body in space.

Further suggestions:

- Begin with stepping then balancing with both feet on each rock, then progress to alternating feet so only one foot at a time is on a river rock.
- Add upside down solid domes to step on in addition to river rocks.

and self-esteem! There are weekend trainings held all over the country to help learn how to teach the program to students. Many teachers in our school are doing Bal-A-Vis-X lessons for 5 minutes a day, up to 15 to 20 minutes a day or several times a week. For further information please feel free to contact me or look up the Bal-A-Vis-X Web site.

I hope this article has inspired you to learn and try some new ideas to provide your students more success in the classroom.

Happy motoring, happy learning!

Helpful Hints

- Be open minded to learn new techniques and strategies to implement in your class.
- Spread your enthusiasm for what you learn, and don't let anything get in your way to implement creative and successful ideas and programs!
- Utilize the various Web sites mentioned to learn more.
- Movement is the foundation for learning; allow your students that opportunity!

References

Goddard, S. (2005). *Reflexes, learning and behavior: A window into the child's mind.* Eugene, OR: Fern Ridge Press.

Oden, A. (2006). *Ready bodies, learning minds.* Spring Branch, TX: David Oden.

56. Brain Exercises

Tammy Haggerty Jones
Sauk Village, Illinois

Recommended Level: Grades K–5

Overall Objective: The student exercises are designed to help rewire the brain, left and right sides, in order to improve concentration, memory, reading, writing, organizing, listening, and physical coordination.

Standards Met (Illinois):

Physical development and health

Materials Needed:

- Crazy straws
- A brick wall
- Chair

- Water
- Fingers
- A smile

I received a phone call from a lifelong friend of my parents in October informing me that I was the recipient of a Notre Dame Alumni Scholarship, and I was asked to attend an "Excellence in Teaching" conference at the University in Indiana (Anzalone, 2006). The topic was "The Brain Rewired," and I wasn't sure if it was designed for me or for my students, but I was excited to learn more.

The timing was perfect. I had been in school with my new third-grade students, 18 boys and six girls, since the middle of August, and I was hosting a student teacher for 14 weeks. Six of my boys had ADHD, and three more were in the early intervention process with medical questions and observation forms for me to complete. I had three bilingual students being mainstreamed and welcomed with smiles and miniphrases from my high school Spanish. Our classroom was filled with energy, spontaneity, diversity, imbalanced gender representation, and twenty-four precious gifts for me to love. Needless to say, a crisp fall weekend on Notre Dame's campus was just what I needed.

The presenter, Ann Anzalone, introduced us to the topic of integrating the left and right sides of the brain through a series of crossover exercises. She discussed the importance of stress management, sleep, nutrition, water, physical activity, memory, and active learning. The purpose of the next three days was to present practical best practices to use in the classroom and create developmentally appropriate lessons for our students. I was ready to learn for my students, and for myself.

We started with a simple exercise, wall push-ups. Ms. Anzalone instructed us to find a wall and stand about 1 foot away with the palms of our hands pressed firmly against it. We were asked to all look right and push 10 times, then left and push 10 times. We repeated this exercise three times.

After 142 of us sat down and began whispering, we learned that the "asymmetrical tonic neck reflex" exercise plays an active role in the learning process and in the development of several cognitive systems. Wall push-ups help create a foundation for the development of hemispheric brain dominance, a reflex responsible for creating the left-hemisphere advantage in speech and language. The exercise coordinates the ears and eyes, and aids with attention and memory.

Hmmm, I thought, let's try this out when I return to school. If you watch any group of school-age children walk down a hall, you will notice constant movement. In my group, I had wonderful children who happened to be arm swingers, toe walkers, hummers, butterfly wing wavers, wigglers, hoppers, and even a boy who spun in circles the entire walk to the bathroom. Waiting in line is boring, and I often find myself in the checkout line still doing the "baby sway," and my son is eleven. I taught my students how to do wall push-ups, and I have noticed a calming effect.

Later that afternoon, our group learned "The Wayne Cook Posture," an exercise designed to reduce anger and relieve stress. Perfect, I thought. I took careful notes.

Sit down and fold your hands. The thumb of the hand that is on top is the ankle to cross on top. (For instance, if your right thumb is on top of your left thumb, cross your ankle with the right one on top.) Extend your arms and cross the arm of which the thumb was on top over the other arm. Point your thumbs down and wave the fingers. Fold your hands, draw them to your chest, and take ten deep breaths. With the tongue on the roof of the mouth breathe in; remove the tongue and breathe out. Uncross your ankles, put your fingertips together, and rest your hands, with the fingertips touching, on your lap. Take ten more breaths.

Ms. Anzalone taught us that anger comes from the brain stem, and breathing through the nose with one hand on the chest and one on the stomach reduces the anger. She also stated that laughter takes "you" out of the brain stem.

I tried this exercise with a child who frequently came to school late, red faced and grizzly. Each time he handed me the crumpled yellow tardy slip, I would smile, say "I'm happy you are here," and begin the brain stem exercise. He would immediately start to laugh, join me, and breathe a sigh of relief. It worked. On the first day, Ann Anzalone taught us that "the brain needs safety and belonging to learn effectively" and "that a teacher's first task is to develop a sense of community." I already knew that!

"The Cross Crawl" integrates both sides of the brain, and if done twice a day, will last for about four hours. My students really enjoy this exercise.

Have the children sit down on their chairs and do 28 puppet movements (touch the elbow of the right arm to the right knee, and then touch the elbow of the left arm to the left knee). Next, have the children do 28 crossover movements (touch the elbow of the right arm to the left knee, and then touch the elbow of the left arm to the right knee). Continue with 14 puppets and 14 crossovers. Now, do 10 puppets and 10 crossovers.

My students like to do the morning session sitting down and the afternoon session standing up with disco, '50s, or hip-hop music playing on the stereo.

One last crossover brain exercise that my students enjoy reminds me of my childhood when I wore a green plaid uniform, knee socks, and saddle shoes—"Here is the church, here is the steeple."

Clasp your hands together with your thumbs crossed in front. Squeeze and feel the fit. If your left thumb is on top, slowly trade so that your right thumb is on top. Do this for each finger, trading one pair at a time until you reach your pinky fingers. Squeeze and feel the odd fit. Now, slowly trade he finger positions back to how they were, beginning with the pinky and ending with the thumbs. Once your students have the hang of it and can trade one finger pair at a time, ask them to complete the process from thumb to pinky and back again three times.

The creators of Brain Gym, Dr. Paul Dennison and his wife Gail Dennison (1989, 1994), devised a formula for water hydration based on research and a simple formula.

Body weight divided by three equals the number of ounces needed daily. Number of ounces divided by eight equals the number of glasses of water needed daily.

The Dennison's also attribute fuzzy short-term memory, trouble with basic math, and difficulty focusing on the printed page and computer screen to a 2% drop in body water.

So, keep your students hydrated, and have them exercise, spin, eat hard candy, use crazy straws, smile, and laugh often. Your students will be smarter for it.

HelpfulTips

- Sleep is important for brain development.
- Spend 15 minutes introducing your students to something new every day. It stimulates the brain.
- Reading helps the brain process, analyze, store, comprehend, and file what was read for use later. Better yet, read aloud and activate two distinct areas of the brain. Speaking activates the motor cortex on both sides, and decoding the words activates one area of the cortex in the left hemisphere.
- Ask your students to draw a smiley face on their schoolwork. A smile balances both sides of the brain.
- A quick way to train yourself and your students to focus is to put your tongue on the bone at the roof of your mouth behind the front teeth and push. Sucking on hard candy also forces you to touch the roof and provides optimum learning.
- Using a crazy straw to drink integrates both sides of the brain and forces the tongue to touch the roof of the mouth.
- Children need to spin, which is why playgrounds, merry-go-rounds, and "Ring-Around-the-Rosie" are popular with children.
- If you have the opportunity to take a Brain Gym class (http://www.braingym.org/schedule?level=1), please sign up. The benefits to your students are worth the investment.

References

Anzalone, A. (2006, October). *The brain rewired.* Presentation given at Excellence in Teaching conference, Notre Dame, IN.

Dennison, P. E., & Dennison, G. E. (1989, 1994). *Brain gym: Teachers' edition.* Ventura, CA: Edu-Kinesthetics.